THE BIBLICAL NAMES OF JESUS

BEAUTIFUL, POWERFUL PORTRAITS OF CHRIST

PAUL THIGPEN

TAN Books
Charlotte, North Carolina

Portions of this book are adapted from the DVD scripts and *Study Guide* text of *Jesus Revealed: Encountering Christ in His Biblical Names* by Paul Thigpen, PhD, and Fr. Jeffrey Kirby, STL (Charlotte, NC: TAN Books, 2017).

Cover design by Caroline K. Green

Cover image: Christ Pantocrator, 13th century, southern gallery of Hagia Sophia, Istanbul (UNESCO World Heritage Site, 1985), Turkey / De Agostini Picture Library / L. Romano / Bridgeman Images

Library of Congress Control Number: 2018956074

ISBN: 978-1-5051-1283-2

Published in the United States by
TAN Books
PO Box 410487
Charlotte, NC 28241
www.TANBooks.com

Printed in the United States of America

For my delightful grandchildren, who are
learning to know, love, and follow Jesus:

Francesco
Sofia
Santiago
Lucia
Avila

"O LORD . . . whose glory above the heavens is
chanted by the mouths of babes and infants."
Psalms 8:1–2

Therefore God has highly exalted him and bestowed on him the name that is above every name, that at the name of Jesus every knee should bow, in heaven and on earth and under the earth, and every tongue confess that Jesus Christ is Lord, to the glory of God the Father.

Philippians 2:9–11

Most merciful Redeemer, friend and brother, let me know you more clearly, love you more dearly, and follow you more nearly. Amen.

Adapted from a prayer ascribed to St. Richard of Chichester (1197–1253)

CONTENTS

IV. PORTRAITS OF JESUS: HIS LIFE IN US

"Who Do You Say That I Am?" An Introduction

"What's in a name? That which we call a rose by any other name would smell as sweet."

This famous question comes from Shakespeare's celebrated play *Romeo and Juliet*. We might be tempted to affirm the romantic sentiment that follows it, spoken by a love-struck Juliet. Her new sweetheart's family name posed an obstacle for their relationship, because his family and hers were enemies. So he could simply change his name, she suggested. A name doesn't really matter so much.

But the people who lived in biblical times would have firmly disagreed.

For many ancient peoples, including the Jews, the name of a person was much more than just a convenient label. A name, properly given and correctly understood, was seen to reflect something important about the person's identity, such as his origins, status, character, deeds, or destiny. It could even in some sense embody the person's essence.

To know someone's name, then, was to know something of that person's identity. In addition, to know a person's name could give a certain access to the person. Then as now, if you knew someone's name, you could address him personally, and using that name affirmed his identity. It gave the two of you a personal connection.

JESUS CHRIST IN SCRIPTURE

The importance of biblical names is nowhere more certain than when we're speaking of Jesus Christ. He is the great, towering figure of the Bible, whose light shines through all its books, those in both the Old Testament and the New. He is the One who stands at the heart of the Scriptures, beckoning us to know him; and knowing him, to love him; and loving him, to follow him—to allow him to make his life our own.

If you search the Scriptures carefully, you'll find more than a hundred names and titles for Jesus. Some were given to him by his family and followers. Some, he claimed for himself. Still others were declared by prophets and psalmists who lived centuries before he was born. Some were even given by angels!

One marvelous way, then, to know, love, and follow him more fully, more truly, is to study his names and titles in Scripture. Each one of them reveals to us some essential aspect of his identity. Taken together, they provide us with a rich, detailed portrait of Jesus Christ: his origins, his status, his character, his deeds, his mission, his destiny.

Each of the eighteen chapters of this book will focus on one of those names or titles, along with others that are closely related. In each chapter, we'll ask: Where is this designation found in Scripture? What does it mean? Most importantly, what does it mean for *us*?

Through these names and titles—if we are willing to reflect deeply upon them—our Lord reveals himself in myriad ways, calling us to know him and love him more deeply.

HOW THIS BOOK IS STRUCTURED

How was Jesus's identity revealed by God to his people? How did they learn about his mission? Long before Jesus was born into our world, God gave them glimpses through prophecies and foreshadowings, received across many generations. But even after Jesus arrived, his contemporaries discovered who he truly was only slowly and gradually.

In the first section of this book, "Portraits of Jesus: His Life on Earth," we will follow their path to discovery. We begin with the names and titles of Christ whose meaning is revealed through the events and circumstances of his earthly life: his conception, birth, and public ministry; his passion and death; his resurrection and his ascension into heaven.

After Jesus returned from earth to heaven, a more complete picture of his identity and mission was gradually revealed by God. Through the words of our Lord, the preaching of the Apostles, and the teaching of their successors—the bishops—the Church broadened and deepened her understanding of Christ.

In the second section of this book, "Portraits of Jesus: His Life in Heaven," we examine how the Scriptures lay a foundation for this richer acquaintance with Jesus. They offer names for him that point to an identity and activity far beyond the few years of his earthly life. Reflecting prayerfully on these names, the early generations of Christians delved deeply into the mystery of Christ's life in heaven with God the Father before all ages, his heavenly reign now, and his return from heaven to earth again one day in glory.

Jesus's mission did not end with his ascension into heaven. Through the Church he established, his mission continues on earth, and his identity is yet more fully revealed.

In the third section of this book, "Portraits of Jesus: His Life in the Church," we consider names and titles of Jesus that point to his saving mission through the Church, his foundational place in the Church, his essential union with the Church, his care and guidance of the Church, and the incomparable Gift of himself to the Church in the Eucharist.

Finally, Jesus came to call each soul into an intimate, personal, eternal relationship with himself. Such a relationship requires a costly commitment from each of his followers, but its rich and everlasting rewards more than compensate for the cost.

In the last section of this book, "Portraits of Jesus: His Life in Us," we reflect on names and titles of Jesus that reveal indispensable aspects of his relationship with each one who answers his call. He shows himself to be our faithful guardian; our source of divine grace; our healing and guiding light; our model and strength; our beginning and our end.

FOR FURTHER REFLECTION

We should note that each chapter concludes with a few aids for further reflection. The biblical references allow for additional study of related scriptural texts. The final words are excerpts from a variety of traditional hymns about Jesus Christ. Our rich heritage of sacred music offers us a treasury of devotional gems that are all too often overlooked or even forgotten when we reflect and pray.

The language of the hymn lyrics may at times seem a bit antique. But we shouldn't let their age keep us from reflecting on their meaning. These poetic words of praise and petition can help us incorporate the biblical insights of each chapter into our conversations with the Lord.

THE MOST CRUCIAL ISSUE

"Who do you say that I am?" (Lk 9:20).

Jesus once asked his disciples this question, and his words ring down the centuries to our day, challenging us as well. In this way he raises the most critical issue we could ever consider.

How shall we answer his question? Our eternal destiny hangs upon our reply.

I

PORTRAITS OF JESUS: HIS LIFE ON EARTH

1

THE WAY, THE TRUTH, AND THE LIFE

*Jesus said to him, "I am the way,
the truth, and the life; no one comes
to the Father, but by me."*

JOHN 14:6

The words of Jesus make it clear that we must name him aright.

Luke's Gospel reports that one day, our Lord is praying alone, and his disciples are with him (Lk 9:18–20). Though we are not told the subject of his prayer, Luke's mention of this detail suggests that what follows has special significance—his action has perhaps been prompted by a directive from his heavenly Father. Jesus turns to the disciples and challenges them with two questions that will press them to understand more clearly who he is and why he has come.

Jesus's first question—"Who do the people say that I am?" (Lk 9:18)—is not the anxious query of someone who worries about what other people think of him. Rather, it reflects the strategy of a wise teacher: He allows the disciples to consider the essential issue of his identity without yet having to answer the question themselves.

The speculations of the people indicate that they recognize our Lord's prophetic authority and activity in his teaching and miracles. But they have failed to grasp who he truly is.

Surely, they think, he must be the fiery prophet John the Baptist, resurrected from the dead after King Herod had him executed (Lk 9:7–9), or perhaps one of the Old Testament prophets raised from the dead. Some think he is even the greatest of the ancient prophets, Elijah, returned to earth after his mysterious departure centuries before on horses and chariots of fire (2 Kgs 2:11–12). Herod has heard the same speculations (Lk 9:7–9). But Jesus is actually none of these.

Now our Lord asks the all-important question, addressed directly to the disciples: "But who do *you* say that I am?" (Lk 9:20, emphasis added). They must answer this question for themselves; they cannot avoid the issue if they are to be his disciples.

As usual, Peter speaks first and on behalf of the others. He replies, "The Christ of God" (Lk 9:20). We will consider the profound meaning of Peter's response in our next chapter. But for now, we can conclude that even though Jesus speaks with God's authority and performs miraculous signs as the great prophets of Israel have done, he is much more than just another teacher or prophet.

Many people today see Jesus as some of his contemporaries did: just a good man, a wise teacher, and nothing more. But such a view fails to consider what Scripture says about him, and most importantly, what he says about himself.

A Farewell Address

The Gospel of John records a later conversation between Jesus and his Apostles, on the night he is betrayed (chapters 14 through 17). He knows his death is at hand, and his last words resemble in form and content the kind of farewell address that we find in several other biblical passages (Jacob to his sons, Gn 49; Moses to Israel, Dt 33; Joshua to Israel, Jo 23–24; and King David to the people of Israel, 1 Chr 28–29).

Like a "last will and testament," the farewell address allows our Lord to make important declarations that must be recorded and remembered. He is summing up those things that he wants to impress deeply on those he loves.

Among the customary elements of the farewell address found in John 14:1–11 are an acknowledgment of a soon departure and words of comfort to those left behind. Jesus reassures his friends that he will "go to prepare a place" for them in the house of his heavenly Father. In time, he will return to take them to himself so that where he is, they also will be (v. 3).

Our Lord is not just promising his followers guidance as a teacher. He is promising them the supreme gift of himself. The ultimate goal of his relationship with them is to have them live at "home" in fellowship with him and his heavenly Father for all eternity.

Some biblical scholars have noted that our Lord's words seem to suggest the imagery of wedding customs of the day. In that culture, the groom would leave his betrothed wife at her home with her parents to go prepare a home for her in his native town. Once the home and the wedding feast were prepared, he would return to escort the bride back there for the feast.

If nuptial imagery is indeed intended here, it's in keeping with Jesus's reference to himself as "the bridegroom" (Mt 9:15; Mk 2:19–20; Lk 5:34–35); his parable of the wise and foolish virgins who await the coming of the bridegroom (who represents Jesus at his second coming, Mt 25:1–13); and John the Baptist's reference to Jesus as the bridegroom (Jn 3:28–29). Similar imagery appears in the description of "the marriage supper of the Lamb" in the Book of Revelation, and a reference to the Church as the "bride adorned for her husband" (Rv 19:9; 21:2). The Lamb and the husband are Christ.

We will say more about this imagery in chapter 12. For now, we should note that all these nuptial references are striking in their portrayal of Jesus's followers, not simply as disciples or even friends, but as those who know him intimately and await a spiritual consummation of their love for him. He is so much more than just a teacher or prophet!

THE WAY, THE TRUTH, AND THE LIFE

When the Apostle Thomas seeks clarity about the way Jesus's followers must take to arrive at such a destiny, Jesus replies: "*I am* the way, and the truth, and the life; no one comes to the Father, but by me" (Jn 14:6, emphasis added). This is a startling claim; no prophet or teacher sent by God has ever spoken this way.

Our Lord is not offering a road map to heaven; he himself *is* the path to that final destination. He has not come simply to speak the truth about God and about humanity. He himself *is* the truth about God and about humanity. He is not simply explaining the meaning of life in its fullness and abundance; he himself *is* that full and abundant life (Jn 10:10).

St. Hilary (c. 310–c. 367), Bishop of Poitiers and a Father and Doctor of the Church, puts it this way: "[Jesus] himself has chosen these winning names to indicate the methods that he has appointed for our salvation. As the way, he will guide us to the truth. As the truth, he will establish us in the life" (*On the Trinity* 7.33).

This kind of claim is different from the claims typically made by the founders of religions. While they see themselves as teachers of wisdom about life, or revealers of God's will, Jesus is calling his followers to encounter *himself* and embrace *himself* as the way, the truth, and the life. His very person is at the center of his message and his mission—the very essence of his message and his mission. And his words imply that those who reject him or ignore him will fail to live abundantly and, in the end, will be lost on the way to the Father's house.

For this reason, Jesus's followers are called above all into a relationship with him: to know him, to place their faith in him, to love him, to serve him. Only such a communion makes possible a true journey to God and a life in and with God.

A LOVE ABOVE ALL OTHERS

In fact, Jesus asks of his followers not just their love, but a love that exceeds all others—even their love for their parents and children. "He who loves father or mother more than me is not worthy of me; and he who loves son or daughter more than me is not worthy of me" (Mt 10:37). He goes so far as to call his disciples to lose their lives for his sake (Mt 16:25).

What might such a relationship with Jesus look like? What

kind of commitment would it require? Some years later, the Apostle Paul describes his own relationship with Christ when writing his letter to the Philippians (3:7–11).

There, he surveys his soon-to-be-completed life and concludes that compared to knowing Jesus, nothing else matters; all else is meaningless without him: "Indeed I count everything as loss because of the surpassing worth of knowing Christ Jesus my Lord. For his sake I have suffered the loss of all things, and count them as refuse, in order that I may gain Christ" (Phil 3:8).

Two Greek words here convey the intensity of Paul's conviction. The one translated as "surpassing worth" (*hyperechon*) asserts that knowing Jesus far excels in value all other things; it is the supreme, the ultimate good. The word rendered here as "refuse" (*skubalon*) means, not simply trash, but the spoiled food thrown out to the dogs, or even dung in the latrine. The Apostle is stretching the limits of language to convey the infinite worthiness of Christ to be the center and purpose of our lives.

Note as well that this is the only time in Scripture when Paul refers to Jesus as "*my* Lord" (Phil 3:8, emphasis added). He makes sure we realize that he is not simply talking about an intellectual awareness of certain facts about Jesus. He is expressing a *personal* knowledge, an *intimate* acquaintance, with Jesus—even though Paul never walked with our Lord during his earthly ministry as the twelve Apostles did.

To "gain Christ," Paul tells us, is a goal that must overshadow all others. It demands our total commitment; no sacrifice is too great to attain that destiny. The Apostle is in fact already demonstrating the sincerity and firmness of his commitment by his willingness to endure prison for preaching about Jesus Christ; he writes to the Philippians from a jail cell (Phil 1:12–14). In the end, he will gladly die for the sake of his Lord. Other Apostles will do the same when confronted with the choice of either rejecting Christ or giving up their lives.

A LOVE ONLY GOD HIMSELF COULD DEMAND

Paul and the other Apostles are Jews. Imagine for a moment how they and their fellow Jews might first respond to our Lord's declarations. They have been taught that such a total commitment, a personal adherence of love, trust, and obedience that supersedes all others, belongs to God alone. "I am the LORD your God," their Creator has said to them when giving them his Law to live by. "You shall have no other gods before me" (Ex 20:2–3). Only the Creator of the universe has the right to make such a demand.

Moses once commanded the ancient Israelites (the ancestors of the Jews): "Hear, O Israel: The LORD our God is one LORD; and you shall love the LORD your God with *all* your heart, and with *all* your soul, and with *all* your might" (Dt 6:4–5, emphasis added). By the time of Jesus, these words are familiar to every devout Jew, who recites them as part of a prayer every morning and evening. It is called the *Shema Yisrael* ("Hear, O Israel") from the opening words of the prayer in Hebrew.

We shouldn't be surprised, then, to find that these words from Deuteronomy are the basis of Jesus's reply to a scribe's question, on another occasion, about which is the greatest commandment of God's law (Mt 22:34–40). At the heart of the Jewish faith is the conviction that the Lord wants *all* of each person's heart, soul, and might (strength) for himself—a total devotion of love.

LONGING FOR GOD

As evidenced in the Psalms, the Jewish people have long prayed fervently that God would enable them to cultivate such a relationship. To do so, he would have to reveal to them the truth about himself, the path that leads to him, and the kind of life that would draw them close to him in friendship.

Psalm 25, attributed to King David (or perhaps written in his honor), expresses such yearning eloquently: "To you, O LORD, I lift up my soul. . . . Make me to know your ways, O LORD; teach me your paths. Lead me in your truth, and teach me, for you are the God of my salvation; for you I wait all the day long. . . . Good and upright is the LORD. . . . He leads the humble in what is right, and teaches the humble his way" (vv. 1, 4–5, 8, 9).

The final destination of these paths, along which the psalmist is led by truth, is "the friendship of the LORD" (Ps 25:14). The Hebrew word translated here as "friendship" is in some versions of the text translated as "secret" or "secret counsel" or even "intimacy." It comes from a root term that refers to those who come together for confidential conversation.

The God who calls his people to himself is not a distant dictator of the universe seeking slaves to do his bidding. He is a God of "compassion" and "merciful love" (Ps 25:6). In our obedience to his gracious will, we find our healing, our freedom, and our salvation from sin.

Psalm 42 provides another example of such holy yearning for God. "As a deer longs for flowing streams, so longs my soul for you, O God. My soul thirsts for God, for the living God" (Ps 42:1–2).

The psalmist's desire is not just for God's gifts or blessings, but for God himself. His longing is so passionate, so fundamental to his being, that it seems instinctive, visceral, physical, a desperate thirst that must be quenched if he is to go on living. His prayer is echoed in the words of King David: "My soul thirsts for you, my flesh faints for you, as in a dry and weary land where no water is" (Ps 63:1). At the time his prayer is spoken, the king is in the Wilderness of Judah, perhaps fleeing from his rebel son, Absalom (2 Sm 15). His physical surroundings are the stark exterior image of an interior reality.

The psalmist wants God to be near, intimate, familiar: "When shall I come and behold the face of God?" (Ps 42:2). A distant God, a hidden God, will not suffice, will not satisfy. "By day the LORD commands his steadfast love; and at night his song is with me, a prayer to the God of my life" (v. 8).

Still other psalmists speak in prayer of their intimacy with God: "I am continually with you; you hold my right hand. You guide me with your counsel, and afterward you will receive me to glory. Whom have I in heaven but you? And there is nothing upon earth that I desire besides you. . . . For me it is good to be near God" (Ps 73:23–25, 28).

JESUS'S CLAIM TO OUR LOVE

Jesus's devout Jewish contemporaries are well aware, then, that God has called them to himself. The truth about him, the way that leads to him, leads to abundant life in his presence. But

God requires that they be fully his if they are to be intimately near him and see his face.

It is in this very context that Jesus tells his followers—whom he will now declare to be no longer his servants, but his friends (Jn 15:15)—"I am the way, and the truth, and the life; no one comes to the Father but by me"; and in the same conversation, "he who has seen me has seen the Father" (Jn 14:6, 9). How can Jesus legitimately make such claims? And how can Jesus ask his followers to love him in the way they should love God alone: more than all others; more than life itself?

The answer to that question is found in his biblical names and titles. So to obtain a more complete picture of his identity and mission, we must search the Scriptures further to discover them. Viewing them together, we can begin to grow in our knowledge of him, faith in him, and love for him, just as his disciples grew in their understanding of the living Mystery who walked among them. We can come to see how Jesus is indeed revealed through them all as the Way, the Truth, and the Life.

SCRIPTURAL PASSAGES TO PONDER

Luke 9:18–20; John 14:1–11; Philippians 3:7–11; Exodus 20:1–3; Deuteronomy 6:4–5; Matthew 22:34–40; Psalms 25:4–14; 42:1–2, 8; 73:23–25, 28

Thou art the Way: to thee alone
From sin and death we flee;
And he who would the Father seek
Must seek him, Lord, by thee.
Thou art the Truth: thy word alone
True wisdom can impart;

Thou only can inform the mind
And purify the heart.
Thou art the Life: the rending tomb
Proclaims thy conquering arm,
And those who put their trust in thee
Nor death nor hell can harm.

FROM GEORGE W. DOANE, "THOU ART
THE WAY: TO THEE ALONE" (ALT.)

2

LION OF THE TRIBE OF JUDAH

"Behold, the Lion of the tribe of Judah,
the Root of David, has conquered."

REVELATION 5:5

God's revelation of Jesus's identity and mission began even before he was conceived. But the revelation unfolded only slowly throughout his lifetime, as its rich and varied aspects became manifest through divinely orchestrated messages and events. A world of mystery surrounded this Man, and things were not always as they seemed, even to some of those who thought they knew him well.

The Jewish people of Jesus's day awaited a promised Messiah-King, or "Anointed One," sent by God, as announced long before in a number of Old Testament passages. In the long process of understanding who Jesus truly was, many of his contemporaries first recognized him as the fulfillment of these Messianic promises. Though he was that and much more, we turn next to his role as Messiah (Christ), because it lies at the core of his identity and mission.

THE CRY FOR A DELIVERER

"How lonely sits the city that was full of people! . . . She weeps bitterly in the night, tears on her cheeks . . . because the LORD has made her suffer for the multitude of her transgressions" (Lam 1:1, 2, 5).

So speaks the prophet Jeremiah in the biblical book of Lamentations. In the sixth century BC, God has permitted a severe chastisement of his people for their sins: an invasion and devastation of the land of Judah by the armies of the Second Babylonian Empire, followed by the forced exile of many. Jeremiah now weeps over the ruins of the capital city of Jerusalem.

In his sorrow, the prophet cries out to God: "Why do you so long forsake us? Restore us to yourself, O LORD. . . . Or have you utterly rejected us?" (Lam 5:20–22).

Jeremiah's heartbroken lament embodies the grief of an entire people. They have submitted themselves to the mastery of sin. So God has submitted them to the mastery of a brutal enemy. The chains they now bear on their bodies reflect the chains that burden their souls.

Yet Jeremiah also speaks for his people when he offers these words of consolation: "But this I call to mind, and therefore I have hope: The steadfast love of the LORD never ceases, his mercies never come to an end; they are new every morning; great is your faithfulness. 'The LORD is my portion,' says my soul, 'therefore I will hope in him'" (Lam 3:21–24).

Despite the many sins of his people, then and now, the

Lord is most certainly merciful. So he promised through the prophets to send someone who would deliver his people from bondage and establish a righteous kingdom that would never end, that could never be overthrown by the powers of evil. Across the generations, this promised Deliverer would be given many names and titles.

THE TRIBE OF JUDAH

In the last chapter, we noted the "farewell address" found in several biblical passages, in which someone near death leaves a kind of "last will and testament" for family and friends. The words in Genesis 49 record the farewell address of the patriarch Jacob (given by God the name "Israel"), Isaac's son and Abraham's grandson. (The dating of the events during this period is uncertain, though many scholars suggest they occurred between 1800 and 1600 BC.)

Jacob is speaking on his deathbed to his twelve sons, from whom the twelve tribes of Israel derive their names. His declarations have a prophetic character, speaking not simply about his sons' future, but also about the future of their descendants, who will form the nation of Israel.

Judah (from whose name come the English words "Jew" and "Judaism") is Jacob's fourth son by his wife Leah (Gn 29:35). Scripture tells us that the name is related to the Hebrew term for "praise" (*Hodah*), because his birth caused Leah to "praise the Lord."

Jacob's deathbed prophecy sets Judah (and by extension, his descendants in the tribe that bears his name) above all the rest of his brothers: "Judah, your brothers shall praise you;

your hand shall be on the neck of your enemies; your father's sons shall bow down before you" (Gn 49:8).

The prophecy also speaks of a future kingdom that someone from the tribe of Judah will rule: "The scepter shall not depart from Judah, nor the ruler's staff from between his feet, until he comes to whom it belongs; and to him shall be the obedience of the peoples" (Gn 49:10). The striking image used to portray Judah in this prophecy is a powerful lion, the king of beasts (v. 9). The lion is an ancient symbol of royalty, majesty, and strength.

This declaration seems to refer at one level to the future dynasty of King David (c. 1010–970 BC), the great monarch of the Jews' ancestral nation. He was Judah's royal descendant, who ruled a united Kingdom of Israel that included all twelve of the tribes descended from Jacob. But it also points to a universal king of "the peoples" (Gn 49:10). Similar prophecies are found throughout later passages of the Old Testament.

KING DAVID'S DESCENDANT

God speaks to King David himself through the prophet Nathan, announcing that this kingdom will endure forever: "Your house [dynasty] and your kingdom shall be made sure for ever before me; your throne shall be established for ever" (2 Sm 7:16).

The divine promise is echoed by the psalmist: "I will sing of your mercies, O LORD, for ever. . . . You have said, 'I have made a covenant with my chosen one, I have sworn to David my servant: "I will establish your descendants for ever, and build your throne for all generations"'" (Ps 89:1, 3–4). Because of these and other biblical passages, the Promised

One to come is eventually known as "the Son of David," meaning the descendant of King David, who belonged to the tribe of his ancestor Judah.

Two centuries later, the prophet Isaiah (eighth century BC) confirms the coming of this king and his everlasting kingdom, declaring that a child will one day be born, "and the government will be upon his shoulder. . . . Of the increase of his government and of peace there will be no end, upon the throne of David, and over his kingdom, to establish it, and to uphold it with justice and with righteousness from this time forth and for evermore" (Is 9:6–7).

God also speaks through the prophet Micah, one of Isaiah's contemporaries, addressing a prophecy specifically to the little village of Bethlehem, King David's birthplace: "But you, O Bethlehem Ephratha, who are little to be among the clans of Judah, from you shall come forth for me one who is to be ruler in Israel, whose origin is from of old, from ancient days" (Mi 5:2).

The prophet Zechariah (sixth century BC) adds his prophetic words about the promised king: "Shout aloud, O daughter of Jerusalem! Behold, your king comes to you; triumphant and victorious is he, humble and riding on a donkey" (Zec 9:9).

THE ANOINTED ONE

Among the ancient Israelites, the ceremony for recognizing a king or priests includes an anointing—that is, the pouring of holy oil upon his head (Ex 28:41; 29:7; 1 Sm 9:16; 15:1; 16:3, 12, 13; 1 Kgs 1:34; 2 Kgs 9:3). This symbolic gesture designates the one anointed as consecrated, or set apart by

God and for God. The custom of anointing has also formed a part of the Christian tradition from the beginning, with oil figuring prominently in some of the sacraments and in the consecrations of certain sacred objects.

In time, the divinely promised king of an everlasting kingdom, descended from Judah (and David, who was of the tribe of Judah), comes to be known as "the Anointed One"; in Hebrew, *Mashiach* (or in English, *Messiah*). In Greek, which became the everyday language of many Jews living in the territories conquered by Alexander the Great (356–323 BC), the title was either written as *Messias* or translated by the Greek term for "the Anointed One," *Christos* (in English, "Christ"). He was called as well "the Son of David," meaning the descendant of King David.

The Jewish people of Jesus's time have developed high expectations for the promised Messiah. In the centuries since King David's reign, their nation has been conquered and occupied by several foreign empires in succession, and their people have been scattered across other nations in exile. The dynasty of David seems to have come to an end.

Even so, through the kingdom of the Messiah to come, they believe, God will reestablish David's dynasty. The Messiah will liberate the Jews from their oppressors, unite the tribes of Israel, bring back to the land of Israel the Jews in exile, and bring about an age of universal peace, prosperity, and recognition of God.

One of the best known of the biblical passages supporting some of these hopes is found in Isaiah 2:1–4, where the prophet declares that "the mountain of the house of the Lord"—that is, Mount Zion, where the Temple stands—"shall be established as the highest of the mountains . . . and all the nations shall flow to it" to worship. "He shall judge between the nations, and shall decide for many peoples; and they shall beat their swords into plowshares, and their spears into pruning hooks; nation shall not lift up sword against nation, neither shall they learn war any more."

Isaiah 11:1–9 speaks as well of "a shoot from the stump of Jesse" (Jesse was King David's father, so this is a poetic reference to a descendant of David), on whom the Spirit of the Lord rests, who will rule in righteousness. In his reign, "the wolf shall dwell with the lamb" in peace, and "the earth shall be full of the knowledge of the Lord as the waters cover the sea" (vv. 1, 2, 4, 6, 9).

So who was this Child? How would he be recognized? Isaiah had given some hints, prophesying that the Messiah would be anointed to preach good news to the afflicted; bind up the brokenhearted; liberate the captives; open the eyes of the blind and the ears of the deaf; enable the lame to walk and the mute to speak (Is 61:1–3). And so the people waited for such a man.

THE ANNUNCIATION AND BIRTH OF CHRIST

At last came the day when God's promise was fulfilled. The archangel Gabriel comes to announce it—but not in a royal palace, or the headquarters of a military general, or even the magnificent temple that had been rebuilt in Jerusalem. He comes instead to the small town of Nazareth, to the home of a humble young woman named Mary, who is to become the mother of Jesus. And the Messianic prophecies help us to understand more fully what the angel is saying to her.

"Hail, full of grace!" he says to her (Lk 1:28). Then Gabriel refers to our Lord by a name and two titles. We will examine these in later chapters. But for now we will focus on one particular statement he makes: "The Lord God will give to him [her son] the throne of his [fore]father David, and he will reign over the house of Jacob [the house of Israel] forever, and of his kingdom there will be no end" (vv. 32–33).

Clearly, the angel is announcing the birth of the long-awaited Messiah, the royal Son of David, whose rule will be universal, and whose kingdom will stand forever. (In passing, we should note that Gabriel's announcement implies that Mary will be the queen mother.) And so it was. In the fullness of time, she bore a Son, and called his name Jesus, as the angel had instructed.

When Jesus is born, the angels that come from heaven to tell the shepherds the good news explicitly call him "Christ" (Lk 2:11). When he is dedicated in the temple a few days later, we find him in the arms of the old man Simeon, who is "looking for the consolation of Israel"—that is, the Messiah—and has received a promise from God that he will not die until he has seen "the Lord's Christ" (vv. 25–26). In Jesus, that promise is fulfilled. Next the aged prophetess Anna encounters the Baby, and she leaves the temple telling everyone that the looked-for "redemption of Israel" has come (vv. 36–38).

This fulfillment of God's Messianic promise also lies behind the episode recorded in Matthew 2:1–6, where the wise men from the East come to Jerusalem, seeking "the one who has been born king of the Jews." Herod, the puppet-king set up by the Romans who forcibly occupy the land, feels threatened by the foreigners' query. Whether or not he believes that the star they have seen is indeed the herald of the Messiah, he wants no rival to his throne.

Herod no doubt fears that reports of their quest could start troublesome rumors and encourage his enemies, who are many. He must preserve his power and status at all costs.

When Herod questions the religious leaders ("chief priests and scribes") in Jerusalem to find out where "the Christ" (Mt 2:4) is to be born, they cite the Messianic prophecy in Micah we have noted: He will be born in Bethlehem (vv. 3–6). And in precisely that little town, we know from both Matthew and Luke, Jesus is born, even though his parents are residents of Nazareth. By divine arrangement, the Roman governor's census has forced them to travel to "the city of David," and the Baby is born soon after they arrive (Lk 2:1–7).

CHRIST AND MESSIAH

From the beginning of his earthly life, then, Jesus is revealed to be the Messiah, the Christ, "the Anointed One." We saw in our previous chapter how Peter's answer to Jesus's question about his identity expresses his conviction about the matter plainly and firmly: He is "the Christ of God" (Lk 9:20). The other disciples come to the same realization at various times. For example, when Andrew first tells his brother, Simon Peter, that he has met Jesus, he declares: "We have found the Messiah" (Jn 1:41), and the two go on to become our Lord's followers.

All four Gospels, when they record Jesus's triumphant entry into Jerusalem before his passion and death, display its significance as a Messianic event (Mt 21:1–5; Mk 11:1–11; Lk 19:28–40; Jn 12:12–15). Both Matthew and John observe explicitly that this event is fulfilling the Messianic prophecy of Zechariah 9:9 that we have already cited. And all four Gospels report how, on that occasion, the crowds hail Jesus in Messianic terms: "Son of David" (Mt 21:9); "Blessed is the kingdom of our father David that is coming!" (Mk 11:10); "the King who comes in the name of the Lord" (Lk 19:38); "the King of Israel" (Jn 12:12).

Even more importantly, Jesus himself claims the title of Messiah. Consider his conversation with the Samaritan woman at the well (Jn 4:1–42). She says to him, "I know that Messiah is coming (he who is called Christ); when he comes, he will show us all things" (v. 25). Jesus replies simply and forcefully, "I who speak to you am he" (v. 25).

We also hear Jesus make the claim implicitly when he reads aloud a Messianic passage from Isaiah in the synagogue of his hometown, Nazareth: "The Spirit of the Lord is upon me, because he has *anointed* me to preach good news to the poor. He has sent me to proclaim release to the captives and recovering of sight to the blind, to set at liberty those who are oppressed, to proclaim the acceptable year of the Lord" (Lk 4:16–19, emphasis added). Then he boldly declares to those assembled: "Today this Scripture has been fulfilled in your hearing" (v. 21).

On another occasion, when John the Baptist sends messengers to Jesus to confirm for them that he is "the One to come" (that is, the Messiah), our Lord cites yet another prophecy of Isaiah declaring that when the Messiah comes, "the eyes of the blind shall be opened, and the ears of the deaf unstopped; then shall the lame man leap like a deer, and the tongue of the mute sing for joy" (Mt 11:2–5; Is 35:5–6).

All these ministries have in fact been performed by Jesus

so that his Messianic claim is verified by his actions, especially the miracles, which are signs from God pointing to his identity and mission. Those who accept his claim challenge those who do not with this question: "When the Christ appears, will he do more signs than this man has done?" (Jn 7:31). In other words, St. Augustine notes, they are saying: "Unless there are two Christs, this is surely the Christ" (*Tractates on the Gospel of John* 31:7). What more evidence do they need that he is the Messiah sent from God?

A SPIRITUAL KINGDOM

Nevertheless, this incident illustrates the conflict among Jesus's contemporaries about his Messianic claims. For many, our Lord's miracles are not enough to convince them that he is in fact the Messiah. They are expecting the Christ to be a powerful political and military leader who breaks the back of the hated Roman conquerors, vanquishes all the enemies of Israel, and rules the nations. They insist that when the Messiah comes, his kingdom of peace and prosperity will be manifested in its fullness immediately.

By the end of his earthly life, however, Jesus clearly has not met such expectations. He has not established a worldly kingdom. Instead, he has established a spiritual one. "My kingdom is not of this world," he says at his trial before the Roman governor, Pontius Pilate (Jn 18:36), who is about to condemn him to death by crucifixion. At that time, Jesus's enemies mock his Messianic claims, believing that the true "King of the Jews" would be annihilating the Romans, not suffering execution at their hands.

Yet even though Jesus's kingdom is spiritual rather than

worldly, it is no delusion, as his adversaries suppose. It is quite real, more profound and long-lasting than any merely political or military regime.

As the king of such a kingdom, Jesus is the mighty deliverer of those in spiritual captivity. Through his teaching and miracles, he brings spiritual freedom to those who come to him. He breaks the power of sin through forgiveness. He heals those who are oppressed by sickness, and he casts out the demonic spirits that keep many of them bound. He even raises the dead, and in doing so, he frees "those who through fear of death [are] subject to lifelong bondage" (Heb 2:15).

Again contrary to many expectations, the kingdom Jesus has established does not arrive in its fullness immediately; it must grow and branch out slowly: "The kingdom of God is like a mustard seed," he insists, "which a man took and sowed in his field; it is the smallest of all seeds, but when it has grown it is the greatest of shrubs and becomes a tree, so that the birds of the air come and make nests in its branches" (Mt 13:31–32).

Since that time, in fulfillment of the ancient prophecies, the kingdom that Jesus established has indeed spread throughout the world, bringing spiritual life and healing to men and women of every tribe and nation who submit themselves to his kingship. In many ways, the earth has become "full of the knowledge of the Lord" (Is 11:9) through the ministry of Christ's Church. In the Church, people come together from all over the globe to worship the God of Israel, just as Isaiah prophesied (Is 2:2–3). In fact, within a few centuries after the time of Jesus, the day even came when the mighty Roman Empire submitted itself, however imperfectly, to Christ as King.

At the same time, Jesus declares that he will one day come to earth a second time, and on that day, the wretched world order that oppresses the human race—not just spiritually, but also physically and socially—will be destroyed forever. As the Messianic king at last performs this other aspect of his promised role, he will judge the nations and punish wickedness (Mt 25:31–46), with all God's enemies placed utterly "in subjection under his feet" (Heb 2:8). Then he will reign over his people in the fullness of peace, when "he will wipe away every tear from their eyes, and death shall be no more, neither shall there be mourning nor crying nor pain any more, for the former things [will] have passed away" (Rv 21:4).

LION OF THE TRIBE OF JUDAH

We began this chapter with a prophecy from the Bible's first book, Genesis, about Jesus's royal reign as a lion, a ruler descended from Judah. So it is fitting that we now conclude this chapter with a prophecy from the Bible's last book, Revelation, which takes up that theme from Genesis. Though Jesus's earthly life was generally characterized by great gentleness, we are told that when he returns, the conclusion of his Messianic mission will display the ferociousness that is necessary to overcome the great evils of this world.

One of the elders in John's vision as recorded in this last book announces, when he sees Jesus reigning from an everlasting throne: "Behold, the Lion of the Tribe of Judah, the Root of David, has conquered" (Rv 5:5). And so he has.

In unexpected ways, then, and on a calendar still hidden from those on earth, Jesus fulfills God's promise of the Messiah. He has established a Messianic kingdom that far surpasses in its worth and its glory the limited benefits of a merely earthly kingdom. In his gracious reign, we see how the divine plan often stymies and overturns our human plans, while bringing us a liberation and a healing beyond our fondest hopes.

Even so, the Messianic kingdom is made possible only at great cost to the Messiah himself. As we will see in our next chapter, the battle with evil was not won with the blood of armies. It was won instead through the blood of Christ himself.

Scriptural Passages to Ponder

Genesis 49:1–2, 8–10; Isaiah 2:1–4; 9:6–7; Psalms 89:1–4; Luke 1:30–33; 4:16–21; Matthew 2:1–6; 21:1–11; Revelation 5:1–5

> *Hail to the Lord's Anointed,*
> *Great David's greater Son!*
> *Hail, in the time appointed,*
> *His reign on earth begun!*
> *He comes to break oppression,*
> *To set the captive free,*
> *To take away transgression,*
> *And rule in equity.*
>
> FROM JAMES MONTGOMERY, "HAIL
> TO THE LORD'S ANOINTED"

3

LAMB OF GOD

*"Behold, the Lamb of God, who takes
away the sin of the world!"*

The prophet Isaiah once gazed down the centuries and saw
the suffering of a sacrificial Victim unlike any other.

"He was despised and rejected by men," the prophet said;
"a man of sorrows, and acquainted with grief; and as one from
whom men hide their faces, he was despised, and we esteemed
him not. Surely he has borne our griefs and carried our sorrows; yet we esteemed him stricken, struck down by God, and
afflicted. But he was wounded for our transgressions, he was
bruised for our iniquities; upon him was the chastisement that
made us whole, and with his stripes we are healed. . . . He was
oppressed, and he was afflicted, yet he opened not his mouth
. . . like a lamb that is led to the slaughter" (Is 53:3–5, 7).

Who is this Man of sorrows foreseen so clearly by Isaiah?
Who is this sacrificial Lamb?

Centuries even before Isaiah's time, the sacrificial lamb

had played a pivotal role in the history of God's people. Yet many of those who reject Jesus as the Messiah fail to understand, as Jesus tells his disciples, that it is "necessary that the Christ [the Messiah] should suffer" (Lk 24:26).

To explain that statement, our Lord must take them through the Old Testament and "interpret to them in all the Scriptures the things concerning himself" (Lk 24:27). God's plan all along has been for the Messiah to offer himself as a sacrifice to redeem the world; his suffering will make possible his kingdom.

We have seen in the last chapter the prophetic passages in the Old Testament that point to the powerful, liberating reign of the Messiah. But other passages are found in Scripture as well that speak of the Messiah's sorrow and suffering. He is a conquering Lion, yes; but he is also a sacrificial Lamb.

BONDAGE IN EGYPT

In our last chapter we spoke of Jacob, Abraham's grandson, called "Israel" by God. The book of Genesis (chapters 37–50) tells us that after a severe famine in Canaan (the land God promised to Abraham and his descendants), Jacob and his sons and their extended families end up settling in Egypt. Jacob's son Joseph, once sold into slavery there, has been promoted by God's favor to become a high-ranking government official in the nation, second only to the king, called the Pharaoh.

Joseph has overseen the stockpiling of grain in preparation for the famine, which has affected Egypt as well as Canaan. So Egypt now has sufficient food supplies, with enough for Jacob's people as well. The Hebrews, as Jacob's descendants come to be called, settle in the region of Egypt called Goshen, where they prosper and multiply (Gn 47:27).

The book of Exodus (chapters 1—11) picks up that story some time later, when a different Pharaoh has come to power who considers the Hebrews a threat to national security. He enslaves them, and they live a miserable existence for several centuries until God raises up a liberator for them, named Moses. Moses demands that Pharaoh free his people and allow them to return to Canaan. But Pharaoh refuses, even after God sends nine plagues on the Egyptians to force the king's hand.

Finally, God sends one last plague that will break Pharaoh's resistance: On a designated night, God warns his people, he will visit each Egyptian home and take the life of the firstborn, including Pharaoh's own. But the Israelites will be spared if they follow the Lord's instructions to prepare for the event.

THE PASSOVER LAMB

The Israelite families are to choose from their flocks a male lamb without blemish, then sacrifice it. They must place some of the lamb's blood on the doorposts and lintel of their homes, then roast the lamb and eat it, along with unleavened bread (bread without yeast) and bitter herbs. When God visits the land to take the life of the firstborn in each household, he will pass over the Israelite households marked by the blood of the lamb (Ex 12:1–28).

On the designated night, the Israelites obey God's command and are spared the plague. But in all the Egyptian households, including Pharaoh's, the firstborn dies. In his great sorrow over the loss of his child, Pharaoh finally relents.

He sets the Israelites free and allows them to leave the country to begin their long journey to their Promised Land (Ex 12:29–42).

God has told the Israelites to be prepared to leave their homes suddenly, dressed to travel as they celebrate the feast of the lamb. This is why the bread must be unleavened: There is no time to complete the long process of kneading dough and allowing it to rise. Now the Israelites realize the reason for God's instructions. Pharaoh wants them out of the country immediately (Ex 12:31–33).

Not long after, Pharaoh regrets his decision—he wants to keep his slave labor—and sends his chariots after the Israelites to stop their exodus from the land. If he is successful, it will mean for the people a return to slavery, and for many, death. But God rescues them by parting the waters of the Red Sea, allowing their escape to the other side on dry ground. When the Egyptians try to follow, the waters return to their place, and Israel's enemies are swept away (Ex 14).

This is the only the beginning of the story of God's providential care for his people. Forty years will be required to prepare them to inherit the land that God has promised them. But our focus in this chapter is on the lamb of the "Passover," as this event came to be called (because the death angel was allowed to "pass over" their homes).

In his instructions surrounding this deliverance, God commands the Israelites to celebrate an annual Passover feast to commemorate their liberation from slavery, their escape from Egypt, and their rescue from death. Every year, each Israelite household is to choose an unblemished male lamb, a year old, and sacrifice it, then eat it with unleavened bread.

This rite is to be observed "as an ordinance . . . forever" (Ex 12:24; Dt 16:1–3).

The death of the Passover lamb has made possible the salvation of God's people from death, and their freedom from bondage. Each year afterward, when at God's command they celebrate the Passover feast, the lamb is slain and eaten as a memorial of that great day when God fulfilled his promise to defend and deliver his people.

A SCARLET PROPHECY

Now it's one thing to take the people out of Egypt. But it's quite another to take the Egypt out of the people. The Israelites, as they come to be called, escape their taskmasters and the deadly visit of the destroying angel. But in their hearts and minds, they still are not free.

After they start out on their demanding trek to the Promised Land, the people are soon looking over their shoulders. They forget how miserable they were in Egypt, and they begin to long for the costly security of the slavery they once knew. Lacking trust in God, they complain that he will let them starve or thirst to death in the wilderness. Even when he provides for their needs in miraculous ways, in a time of uncertainty they turn to a false Egyptian god, whose idol is a golden calf, and they worship it with riotous and immoral abandon.

Through Moses, God gives them the Law to show them the path to life—if they can keep it. But across the coming generations, one tragic reality is demonstrated to them again and again: The Law is good, but it is not enough in itself to save them from spiritual bondage to the sin that leads to death. God in his grace will have to extend his saving mercy and visit them in a new way.

So the blood of the Passover lamb becomes more than a memorial of what God has done for his people in the past. It becomes as well a scarlet prophecy of what God will do for them one day in the future, to save them from the bondage and death brought on by their sins. To redeem them, to obtain their forgiveness and reconciliation with himself—a price they themselves could never pay—God will shed the blood of a Lamb so precious that it can purchase eternal life for the whole world.

AN OFFERING FOR SIN

The ancient Scriptures provide evidence that sacrificial lambs and their blood serve as a "peace offering," a "sin offering," or a "guilt offering," to "make atonement" for sinners (Lv 3:6–8; 4:32; 5:6; 14:21). Giving up an "unblemished" lamb to God, and shedding its blood, offers a dramatic symbol of the spiritual reality that "the wages of sin is death" (Rom 6:23), and that in the end, only the offering of an innocent life in our stead can cleanse the guilt of our sin. Through the death of an innocent victim, sacrificed on our behalf, comes our atonement with God—our being reunited to him—and our peace with God is restored.

Even so, as the book of Hebrews declares, though "in these sacrifices there is a reminder of sin year after year," the blood of animals in itself cannot take away sin. Rather, as part of God's law for the Jewish people given through Moses, they provide "a shadow of good things to come" (Heb 10:1–4).

They point to a perfectly innocent Victim whose blood can in fact take away the sin of the world.

The prophet Isaiah speaks more explicitly of the profound reality foreshadowed by the sacrificial lamb. In a prophecy that Jesus's followers would later recognize as Messianic, he predicts that the LORD will bare "his holy arm before the eyes of all the nations"—a poetic description of God revealing his power to those who do not know him; "all the ends of the earth will see the salvation of our God" (Is 52:10). Then the prophet goes on to describe a suffering servant who will one day be exalted and recognized by the nations. In him, the Gentiles (non-Jews) will see the fulfillment of divine promises that had never been told to them, and they will come to understand divine mysteries that they had never even heard about before (vv. 13–15).

"To whom has the arm of the Lord been revealed?" (Is 53:1). Isaiah answers that question in the passage we just cited when he tells of a Servant-Messiah who will be "despised and rejected by men, a man of sorrows, and acquainted with grief" (v. 3). He will bear our griefs and carry our sorrows; he will be wounded for our transgressions and bruised for our iniquities. His chastisement will make us whole, and by his bloody stripes from the lash, we will be healed (vv. 4–5).

"All we like sheep have gone astray," the prophet declares, "we have turned every one to his own way; and the Lord has laid on him the iniquity of us all" (Is 53:6). Then the image of the sacrificial lamb is made explicit: The Servant-Messiah is "like a lamb that is led to the slaughter," who "makes himself an offering for sin" (vv. 7, 10).

A CONCRETE PROPHECY

The Passover lamb, then, and all the other sacrificial lambs offered by the Jewish people through the centuries, not only point back in time as a memorial. They also point forward in time to Someone to come. His sacrificial death and suffering will take away sin and heal its wounds in a way that the mere blood of animals could never accomplish.

This annual Passover feast is still being observed, centuries later, in the time of Jesus. The sacrificial lamb offered to God and consumed in a sacred meal has become an age-old reminder that God was and is and will be faithful and powerful to rescue his people from bondage and death.

The Gospel of Luke tells us that as devout Jews, Joseph and Mary make a pilgrimage to Jerusalem each year to celebrate the Passover feast (Lk 2:41). He provides a glimpse of Jesus joining them for that pilgrimage when he is twelve (vv. 41–51). The sacrifice of the Passover lamb, and the fellowship around the meal at the heart of the festival, is for him a lifelong practice (Jn 2:13; 6:4; 11:55–56). He is of course intimately familiar also with the other sacrificial lambs prescribed in the Law of Moses, which are still offered in his time as well.

Those of Jesus's Jewish contemporaries who are accustomed to obeying the divine laws are no doubt aware as well of the laws' origins and significance. So we can imagine their surprise when one day they hear St. John the Baptist, pointing to Jesus in the crowds gathered for baptism in the Jordan, crying out: "Behold the Lamb of God, who takes away the sin of the world" (Jn 1:29–39). Not just the sin of the Jewish people, but the sin of the world! The next day, John repeats his declaration to two of his followers: "Behold the Lamb of God" (v. 35).

ISAIAH'S PROPHECY FULFILLED

John is announcing the fulfillment of Isaiah's prophecy. Here at last stands the Man foreseen by Isaiah, the Suffering Servant, the sacrificial Lamb. Jesus is the Man of sorrows, acquainted with grief, who will bear our griefs and carry our sorrows. He will be wounded for our transgressions, bruised for our iniquities.

Upon him will be laid the chastisement that will make us whole, and with the bloody stripes on his back, we will be healed. He will offer his life for the world, a sacrifice to God that will cleanse the people of their sins. He will take their punishment upon himself and restore their peace with God.

When the time finally arrives for Jesus to give up his life, even more details of his passion and death fulfill Isaiah's prophecy. He is despised by his enemies and unjustly reckoned as a sinner who deserves the punishment he is receiving; they see him as someone "smitten by God" (Is 53:4). At critical times in his multiple trials, he remains silent instead of trying to defend himself (v. 7). His grave is "with the wicked"—he dies between two criminals—and he is "with a rich man in his death" (v. 9)—buried in the personal tomb of the wealthy man Joseph of Arimathea (Mt 27:57–60).

Jesus's passion and death also fulfill prophecies found in a number of other Old Testament passages. Among these, perhaps the most striking are found in Psalm 22, whose opening words Jesus cries out from the cross: "My God, my God, why have you forsaken me?" (Ps 22:1; Mt 27:46).

The psalm tells of the speaker's great trials: the mockery shouted by his enemies (Ps 22:7–8); the brutish men ("bulls") surrounding him who seek his death (v. 12); the evil "dogs" (the Jews called Gentiles "dogs") who pierce his hands and feet (v. 16); his garments divided and distributed by casting lots (v. 18); and various bodily torments (vv. 14–15). All these prophetic references are in keeping with the details of Jesus's crucifixion (Mt 27:32–46; Lk 22:32–37; Jn 19:23–42).

THE APOSTLES COME TO UNDERSTAND

Even for our Lord's closest friends, the notion that his suffering and death is part of his Messianic role is difficult to accept. On one occasion, Jesus tells his disciples that he must "suffer many things . . . and be killed" (Mt 16:21). But Peter actually rebukes him, saying, "God forbid, Lord! This shall never happen to you" (v. 22). Jesus must correct him with a stinging reprimand (v. 23).

Nevertheless, in looking back on all these events, Jesus's disciples come to realize that "it was necessary that the Christ should suffer these things" (Lk 24:26). When the Apostles and other disciples of the Lord preach the gospel after his resurrection, they finally connect the dots between these prophecies and the events of his life.

The Apostle Philip, for example, helps an Ethiopian who is reading the passage about the lamb that we have cited from Isaiah. Philip identifies the suffering servant as Jesus (Acts 8:26–35). In his first epistle, the Apostle Peter reminds his readers that they are ransomed from slavery to sin by the precious blood of Christ, like that of "a lamb without blemish or spot" (1 Pt 1:18–19). The Apostle Paul tells the Christians in the city of Corinth: "Christ, our Passover Lamb, has been sacrificed" (1 Cor 5:7).

THE LAMB IN THE BOOK OF REVELATION

Perhaps the most beautiful and powerful depiction of our Lord as the Lamb of God is found throughout the book of Revelation (Rv 5:6–14). In his vision of heaven, John reports seeing "a Lamb standing, as though it had been slain" (v. 6). This same Lamb is identified by John as "the Lion of the tribe of Judah, the Root of David" (v. 5). As we have seen in the previous chapter, these titles clearly identify him as the Messiah. The Lamb of God and the Lion of Judah are one and the same.

Those in heaven sing the Lamb's praise, declaring to him: "You were slain and by your blood you ransomed men for God from every tribe and tongue and people and nation, and have made them a kingdom and priests to our God, and they shall reign on earth. . . . Worthy is the Lamb who was slain, to receive power and wealth and wisdom and might and honor and glory and blessing!" (Rv 5:9–12).

They are singing about the Messianic kingdom that, in the end, will bring all other kingdoms to an end, when Christ has conquered his enemies and rules as King of heaven and earth. "The kingdom of the world has become the kingdom of our Lord and of his Christ, and he shall reign for ever and ever" (Rv 11:15).

Next, John offers comfort and hope to those of his contemporaries who are suffering persecution and even martyrdom because of their faith in Christ and their love for him. He recognizes that Satan is behind such persecution, trying to tyrannize God's people by enticing them into the slavery of sin and terrifying them by the threat of death. But Satan's defeat has been secured by the sacrificial death of the Lamb, just as Pharaoh's defeat was accomplished by the blood of the Passover lambs.

"And I heard a loud voice in heaven saying, 'Now the salvation and the power and the kingdom of our God and the authority of his Christ have come, for the accuser of our brethren [Satan] has been thrown down, who accuses them day and night before our God. And they have conquered him by the blood of the Lamb and by the word of their testimony, for they loved not their lives, even unto death'" (Rv 12:10–11).

POWER TO CLEANSE AND CONQUER

The blood of the eternal Passover Lamb of God, Jesus Christ, has the power not only to cleanse, but to conquer. He who is perfectly innocent, blameless, without any sin of his own, has taken on himself the misery that we ourselves have merited through our sin. Whoever is washed in that precious blood is strengthened in faith, hope, and love to spurn Satan's entice-ments and to dismiss his threats as the empty taunts of an enemy whose doom is sure.

If his blood, poured out from the Cross, is over the doors of our hearts, eternal death can pass over us; the bondage of sin can be broken; and we can pass through the waters of Baptism on our journey to heaven, our promised homeland. Through the forgiveness that Jesus offers, we can have the peace of reconciliation with God.

And so we pray, with great fervor and longing, at every Mass: *Lamb of God, you take away the sins of the world; have mercy on us. Lamb of God, you take away the sins of the world;*

have mercy on us. Lamb of God, you take away the sins of the world; grant us peace.

Even so, how can the blood of one man become the ransom for the whole world? How can his death bring life to the human race? To understand the mysterious power of the Lamb, we must consider still more of his names and titles.

SCRIPTURAL PASSAGES TO PONDER

Exodus 12:1–14; John 1:29–39; Isaiah 53:1–12; Acts 8:26–35; 1 Peter 1:13–21; 1 Corinthians 5:6–8; Revelation 5:6–14; 12:10–12

At the Lamb's high feast we sing
Praise to our victorious King!
Who hath washed us in the tide
Flowing from his pierced side;
Praise we him whose love divine
Gives his sacred Blood for wine
Gives his Body for the feast
Christ, the Victim, Christ, the Priest!

FROM "AT THE LAMB'S HIGH FEAST WE SING"

4

FIRSTBORN OF THE DEAD

Grace to you and peace ... from Jesus Christ
the faithful witness, the first-born of the dead.

REVELATION 1:4–5

I was a teenage atheist. In those young, rebellious years, I denied the existence of God, of the soul, of any kind of life after death.

I usually kept these skeptical thoughts to myself. But for six long years, I was haunted by the thought: *Life is meaningless. All hope is in vain. One day I will die, and that will be the end of me. I will cease to exist. Day by day, the entire human race, one by one, will do the same. So what's the point of it all?*

Death was a cruel specter that shadowed me—until, that is, I met the Man who rose from the grave, who conquered death: the Firstborn of the Dead.

"Sin came into the world through one man," the Apostle Paul observes, "and death through sin, and so death spread to all men because all men sinned" (Rom 5:12). The early chapters of the book of Genesis recall the sin of our first parents,

Adam and Eve, and the horrors that came in its aftermath. When they rebelled against the Source of Life himself, how could they escape dying?

The generations to come would live out their days under the fearful, sorrowful shadow of death. But God had a plan all along to heal that ancient wound of the human race and to conquer death. He would send his Messiah, not only to suffer and die, but to rise again. "The firstborn of the dead" would open the doors to a new and everlasting life.

A LIFE-GIVING BANQUET

Since ancient times, the feast has been a popular symbol of joy, abundance, and fellowship. After speaking of God's coming triumph over his enemies, the prophet Isaiah describes the victory banquet that the Lord spreads to celebrate, not just for the Jewish people, but "for all peoples a feast of fat things, a feast of choice wines—of fat things full of marrow, of choice wines well refined" (Is 25:6). The "fat" suggests delicious flavor; the "marrow," rich nourishment; and the "wines," merriment.

St. Cyril of Alexandria (c. 376–444) and other ancient Christian writers see in this passage a prophetic reference to the Eucharist, the banquet that God will one day spread for all peoples, bringing them joy, abundant life, and fellowship with him in Christ: "By 'wine' Isaiah points to the mystical Sacrament," he notes, "that of the unbloody Sacrifice, which we celebrate in the holy churches" (*Commentary on Isaiah,* 25:6–7).

What divine victory is celebrated in this life-giving Banquet? God's conquest of death itself—what the Apostle

Paul will later call "the last enemy to be destroyed" (1 Cor 15:26). "And he will destroy on this mountain the covering that is cast over all peoples, the veil that is spread over all nations. He will swallow up death for ever; and the LORD God will wipe away tears from all faces, and the reproach of his people he will take away from all the earth, for the LORD has spoken" (Is 25:7–9).

The "covering" here brings to mind a shroud, the cloth wrapped around a dead body. The "veil" suggests the veil worn by women in mourning. Death will be destroyed, as a cloth rotted by exposure to sunlight finally falls apart into broken threads.

ANCIENT BELIEFS ABOUT DEATH

Ancient peoples offered a variety of speculations about what happens to the human person after death. Some insisted that no part of a person survives death; death is the end; there is no afterlife. Others held that the spirit or soul (the aspect of human nature that gives life to the matter of the body but is not composed of matter itself) survives death but remains forever without a body—what we would call a ghost.

The Jewish people received a gradual revelation from God about the reality of life after death. The earliest believers in the God of Israel seem to have been unaware of human survival after death; little is said explicitly about it in the earliest Hebrew Scriptures. In time, however, there appeared vague references to *Sheol,* a dark, shadowy, underworld abode of the dead (such as Prv 7:27).

In later centuries, many Jews came to believe that Sheol had separate compartments for the righteous dead and the unrighteous dead, and that the latter was a place of punishment. In the book of Daniel we find at last an explicit reference to the resurrection of the dead—that is, the affirmation that the human soul will at the end of time be reunited to the body from which it was separated at death (Dn 12:1–3).

In Jesus's day, Jewish believers remain in disagreement about the survival of the human person after death. The religious sect known as the Sadducees deny the existence of human life after death. Their religious rivals, the sect known as the Pharisees, affirm both post-death survival and the resurrection of the bodies of the dead. The Pharisees' position seems to be the most popular at the time, and Jesus himself affirms the truth of their teaching on the matter.

By the time Jesus begins his public ministry, he is no stranger to death. The Gospels never mention St. Joseph after Jesus was twelve years old. So we can assume that our Lord's beloved foster father has been wrapped away in a shroud by the time the Boy is grown.

THE RAISING OF LAZARUS

Consider as well that poignant scene in Bethany, where Jesus stands at the tomb of Lazarus, weeping over the loss of his dear friend, whose corpse has already begun to decay (Jn 11:1–44). Our Lord's most striking claims about life after death and the resurrection of the body are found in this account.

The story begins when Jesus hears that Lazarus, his beloved friend, lies critically ill and close to death in another town. His sisters send word for the Lord to come, because he has demonstrated that he can miraculously heal the sick. But Jesus remains where he is for another two days, and Lazarus dies.

Jesus then says to his disciples: "Our friend Lazarus has fallen asleep, but I go to awake him out of sleep" (Jn 11:11). They fail to realize that he is speaking figuratively: Lazarus is dead, but Jesus will bring him back to life.

This miracle will demonstrate that Jesus has power, not just over illness and infirmity, but even over death itself. As a result, the Apostles and the other witnesses will have their faith in Jesus strengthened.

Lazarus's two sisters, Martha and Mary, are understandably wondering why Jesus has delayed in coming. When he arrives, Martha says to him, "Lord, if you had been here, my brother would not have died." Yet her confidence in the Lord's power to raise the dead remains firm: "And even now I know," she tells him, "that whatever you ask from God, God will give you" (Jn 11:21–22).

Martha recognizes Jesus's special relationship with God, both as a prophet and as the Messiah. The greatest of the Old Testament prophets, Elijah, once prayed that a young man would be raised from the dead, and his prayer was answered (1 Kgs 17:17–24). So Martha's statement suggests that she considers Jesus to have a similarly exalted prophetic status.

But Jesus wants Martha to understand his unique identity more fully. He presses her: "Your brother will rise again" (Jn 11:23).

Martha replies: "I know that he will rise again in the resurrection at the last day" (Jn 11:24).

Then our Lord makes a claim that no doubt startles and perplexes Martha: "*I am* the resurrection and the life; he who believes in me, though he die, yet shall he live, and whoever lives and believes in me shall never die. Do you believe this?" (Jn 11:25–26, emphasis added).

"I AM THE RESURRECTION AND THE LIFE"

Jesus is not just claiming to be a prophet who raises the dead through prayer, or a wise teacher who reveals the truth about the final resurrection of the dead. He himself *is* the resurrection; he himself *is* the new life of those who rise from the dead. Apart from him, there is no resurrection to eternal life.

Those who adhere firmly to Jesus in faith, he insists, will be raised to new life in him after they conclude their days in this life. And these same adherents will never die in the sense of suffering the "second death" (Rv 2:11; 20:6, 14; 21:8)— that is, eternal separation from God, the very Source of life, a fate that the book of Revelation describes figuratively but soberly as everlasting torment in "the lake of fire" (20:14).

No doubt Martha still has much to understand about Jesus's identity as "the resurrection and the life." But she responds to his question with a simple declaration of faith: "Yes, Lord, I believe . . ." (Jn 11:27).

After entering the tomb where Lazarus has been dead for four days, Jesus weeps and prays. Moments later, before the tears can dry, we hear his voice thundering across that vast, ancient chasm between this world and the next. He overrules death's judgment. He claims for himself death's prey.

"Lazarus!" he commands. "Come forth!" And death must let him go.

The dead man's departed soul hurries back again to his body. Lazarus comes forth from the tomb, grave clothes and all—and the mourners, terrified and amazed, hasten to set him free from his shroud. In this miracle, the witnesses behold "the glory of God" displayed (Jn 11:38–44).

RAISED TO ETERNAL LIFE

We should consider for a moment that Lazarus will not go on to live forever in this world. He will one day die again when his appointed time comes for his personal judgment by God (Heb 9:27). For the time being, then, he has been restored to an earthly life of the kind he had before he died.

Lazarus has been raised, but Lazarus is not the "firstborn of the dead." He returns to this present life, stronger, wiser, jubilant, with a hair-raising story to tell. Even so, he has not yet had his birthday into eternal life. Jesus, who is himself "the resurrection and the life," will be the "firstborn of the dead."

The raising of Lazarus from the dead is of course a stunning sign of Jesus's authority over death. But Lazarus is not yet experiencing the kind of eternal life that Jesus is promising those who believe in him.

If we wish to know something of that kind of life, we must turn to Jesus's own resurrection after his redemptive suffering and death as the Lamb of God, for the kind of resurrection we are promised is the kind he himself experienced: "If we have been united with him in a death like his," the Apostle Paul teaches, "we shall certainly be united with him in a resurrection like his" (Rom 6:5).

We must recognize that the kind of resurrection Jesus promises us leads to an everlasting life; we will not die a second time as Lazarus did. Paul continues: "If we have died with Christ, we believe that we shall also live with him. For we know that Christ being raised from the dead will never die again; death no longer has dominion over him" (Rom 6:8–9).

Because Jesus has brought Lazarus back from the dead,

Death now knows who is Boss. But he bides his time, hoping for the chance to exact his revenge.

THE RESURRECTION OF CHRIST

The day finally comes when Death will make his move. On that dark Friday morning when the sun hides his face, when the nails are driven into the cross, when the blood and water run down like a river, when Jesus cries out in his final agony, "It is finished!"—Death closes his jaws upon that thorn-crowned head, exulting that he has finally conquered his Enemy (Jn 19:30).

The precious Body is taken down from the cross, wrapped in its own shroud, laid to rest hurriedly in a borrowed tomb. The crucified Victim's mother takes on her veil, her face awash in a sea of tears. We can imagine Death sneering and boasting in a rasping whisper: "So has it ever been and ever shall be. In the end, no man escapes from me!"

No mere man, that is. No mere mortal. But this Man, this Jesus, is no mere mortal. Eternal life, the very life of God, flows through him. His bodily life was not taken from him against his will. He himself chose to lay it down to redeem the world; and through irresistible, invincible divine power, he will take it up again.

Dawn approaches on Sunday morning. God the Father speaks once again into the darkness, as he did when he first created the world. Once again, on the morning of the first day of the week, in the silent blackness of the tomb, he commands, "Let there be light!"

And from the dark womb of a dying world the light of eternity breaks forth. A New Creation is born that transcends the first creation (2 Cor 5:17). Jesus Christ rises from the dead, never more to die: the "firstborn of the dead," the Head of the New Creation.

He has tasted death for each one of us—and he has swallowed it up in victory.

Jesus Christ is Life himself. How could death possibly hold on to such a prey? Christ first submits to death so that he might vanquish death. He turns the enemy's weapon against the enemy himself.

Like some new David, the young shepherd of old, Jesus confronts the ancient, boastful Goliath of death, the terror of all men. Then he brings him down and finishes him off with the Giant's own sword.

St. Augustine can hardly contain himself as he speaks of this glorious mystery: "The One who is our very life," he exclaims, "descended into our world, and bore our death, and slew it with the abundance of his own life! . . . Sons of men, how long will you be so slow of heart? Now that Life himself has descended to you, won't you ascend [with him] and live?" (*Confessions* IV.12).

CHRIST'S RESURRECTED BODY

All the Gospels report eyewitness accounts of the empty tomb after Jesus rises from the dead, and of his later appearances to them (Mt 28:1–10, 16:20; Mk 16:1–19; Lk 24:1–53; Jn 20:1–29; 21:1–24). The details of his disciples' encounters with the risen Christ demonstrate that the life flowing through his resurrected body is not simply a restoration of the kind of bodily life we usually experience in this world.

No doubt the body Jesus has is truly his own. It bears scars from the wounds of his passion and death. It is not simply an apparition. His disciples are able to touch it, and he eats food while they watch to prove that he is not an illusion or even a disembodied spirit (Lk 24:36–42). Nevertheless, Jesus's body is able to pass through closed doors, appearing and disappearing as his disciples watch (Lk 24:31, 36–37; Jn 20:19–20, 26). He also seems to be able to keep friends from recognizing him (Lk 24:15–16).

These qualities of our Lord's resurrected body are indications of a new quality of life in his human nature, a transformation that will take place in our human natures as well at the final resurrection of those who are in Christ. The Apostle Paul promises that "the Lord Jesus Christ . . . will change our lowly body to be like his glorious body" (Phil 3:20–21).

In another letter (1 Cor 15:12–20), Paul compares our death and resurrection to the transformation of a seed that has been planted and then springs up in new life: "So it is with the resurrection of the dead. What is sown is perishable; what is raised is imperishable. It is sown in honor; it is raised in glory. It is sown in weakness; it is raised in power" (vv. 42–43).

In this same passage, Paul goes on to echo the words from Isaiah we have just read. The prophet says that God "will swallow up death forever" (Is 25:8). The Apostle announces, "When the perishable puts on the imperishable, and the mortal puts on immortality, then shall come to pass the saying that is written: 'Death is swallowed up in victory'" (1 Cor 15:54). He sees in Jesus's resurrection, and the promise of our resurrection in him, the fulfillment of the ancient prophecy that death will be destroyed.

"DEATH SHALL BE NO MORE"

In a similar way, Isaiah's words "The LORD God will wipe away tears from all faces" (Is 25:8) are echoed in the book of Revelation: "God will wipe away every tear from their eyes" (Rv 7:17); "death shall be no more" (21:4).

In fact, throughout the book of Revelation, Jesus appears as the glorious Vanquisher of death, whose triumphant resurrection has given him authority over this ancient enemy of the human race, to set at liberty those it has held captive. He announces: "Fear not, I am . . . the living one; I died, and behold I am alive for evermore, and I have the keys of Death and Hades [the realm of the dead]" (1:17–18).

We can understand, then, why John, in reporting his vision, would call Jesus "the first-born of the dead" (Rv 1:5). He is the "first-born" of many brothers and sisters in the new family of God (Rom 8:29) who pass through death, like the darkness of a womb, and emerge into the light of a new life in heaven.

This is why, since ancient times, Christian writers have spoken of the day on which a faithful believer dies as that person's "birthday" into eternity. Just before his martyrdom, St. Ignatius of Antioch (died c. 107) alludes to that conviction when he declares: "The birth pangs are upon me" (*Epistle to the Romans,* 6:1).

Note that in all these biblical passages, we are focusing on God's promise of conquering death through new life and the resurrection of the body. Understanding who Jesus is, and who he is for us, shows us that such hope is firmly grounded: "As Christ was raised from the dead by the glory of the Father, we too [can] walk in newness of life" (Rom 6:4). In chapter

10, our focus will turn to the meaning of this eternal life in Christ—what it is to live with him forever in his "Father's house" (Jn 14:2).

"O DEATH, WHERE IS YOUR STING?"

I have lived a long life now, and I am no stranger to death. I have buried more loved ones than I care to count; not long ago, my best friend was suddenly taken from me. With every evening, my own passing draws nearer than before.

But I am no longer an atheist. I know now beyond all doubt that death is not the end. It is only a beginning, a birthday into eternity for all those who belong to the One who is the Resurrection and the Life, the Firstborn of the dead. He is risen, and by God's grace, we will rise with him to everlasting life.

For this reason, I can declare triumphantly with St. Paul: "O death, where is your victory? O death, where is your sting? . . . Thanks be to God, who gives us the victory through our Lord Jesus Christ!" (1 Cor 15:55, 57).

SCRIPTURAL PASSAGES TO PONDER

Exodus 12:1–14; John 1:29–39; Isaiah 53:1–12; Acts 8:26–35; 1 Peter 1:13–21; 1 Corinthians 5:6–8; Revelation 5:6–14; 12:10–12

> *The strife is o'er, the battle done,*
> *The victory of life is won;*
> *The song of triumph has begun: Alleluia!*
> *The powers of death have done their worst,*
> *But Christ their legions hath dispersed.*

Let songs of holy joy outburst: Alleluia!
Lord, by the stripes which wounded thee,
From death's dread sting thy servants free,
That we may live and sing to thee: Alleluia!

FROM "THE STRIFE IS O'ER, THE BATTLE WON"

II

PORTRAITS OF JESUS: HIS LIFE IN HEAVEN

5

KING OF KINGS

He is Lord of lords and King of kings.

REVELATION 17:14

The role of Messiah, as we have seen, is at its heart a royal role. The Christ is to be seated on King David's throne as the promised ruler of Israel, whose rule will extend worldwide to judge the nations, and whose kingdom will last forever.

We might be able to envision such a king with a reign limited to human history: a kind of global emperor whose dynasty manages to survive with God's help, generation after generation, until the very last generation of the human race. But we have seen that the kingship of Jesus Christ "is not of this world" (Jn 18:36). Titles of Jesus such as "King of kings," "Lord of lords," and "King eternal" press us to recognize that the Messiah's reign is far beyond any kingdom possible for someone who rules only within human history.

To begin to understand Christ's reign in its fullness, we must turn our eyes toward heaven.

THE MESSIAH'S GLORY

We have noted how, after his passion, death, and resurrection, Jesus tells his disciples that it was "necessary that the Christ should suffer these things." But his sentence doesn't end there. The Messiah had to suffer these things, he explains, "and *enter into his glory*" (Lk 24:26, emphasis added).

In New Testament Greek, the word translated here as "glory" (*doxa*) means "brilliance, splendor, radiance." Often it is used to describe those who dwell in heaven (Heb 9:5; Lk 2:9; Acts 7:2; 1 Cor 15:43; Col 3:4; 2 Thes 1:9; 2 Pt 1:17; Rv 15:8; 19:1; 21:11, 23).

By extension, "glory" also refers to the magnificence, exaltation, praise, and splendor belonging to someone on account of his known excellence. In this sense, St. Augustine defines glory as "brilliant celebrity with praise."

How did Jesus "enter into his glory"? We find glimpses of his glory even as he walks the earth, most notably in his brilliant transfiguration on the mountaintop, when "his face shone like the sun, and his garments became white as light" (Mt 17:1–8). But these are only a foretaste of the glory he enters when, after his resurrection, he ascends into heaven.

The Gospel of Matthew tells us that just before our Lord ascends, he tells his disciples that "all authority in heaven and on earth" has been given to him by God (Mt 28:16–20)—the ultimate exaltation and recognition. Then, according to the Gospel of Luke, Jesus is "carried up into heaven" (Lk 24:51).

What happens there? The Gospel of Mark adds that after Jesus is taken up into heaven, he sits down "at the right hand of God" (Mk 16:19). In ancient times, to be positioned "at the right hand" of an enthroned sovereign means to assume a place of highest honor, and often a share in his rule. In ancient Israel, for example, the queen sat at the right hand of the king (2 Kgs 2:19; Ps 45:9).

In the book of Acts, we catch a glimpse of Jesus at the right hand of God's throne. When the deacon Stephen is about to be stoned by a mob for preaching Jesus, he reports a vision of heaven. He sees "the glory of God, and Jesus standing at the right hand of God" (Acts 7:54–56). In his exaltation, Jesus is once again sharing the glory of his Father: his magnificent splendor, and the adoring praise of all those in heaven.

A PORTRAIT OF CHRIST'S EXALTATION

The Apostle Paul speaks further of Christ's exaltation to glory in heaven. He prays that the Christians in the city of Ephesus will be enlightened to understand more fully "the immeasurable greatness of [God's] power in us who believe, according to the working of his great might which he accomplished in Christ when he raised him from the dead and made him sit at his right hand in the heavenly places, far above all rule and authority and power and dominion, and above every name that is named, not only in this age, but also in that which is to come; and he has put all things under his feet" (Eph 1:18–23).

We should note that on his throne in heaven, Jesus is not simply reigning as King of the universe. He is also our advocate before God, as Paul reminds us: "Christ Jesus, who died, yes, who was raised from the dead, who is at the right hand of God, who indeed intercedes for us" (Rom 8:33; also Heb 7:25).

What a marvelous reality to ponder, bringing us powerful consolation. The Son of God incarnate retains his human nature forever; he did not cast it away when he ascended into heaven. The One who intercedes with the Father for us intimately knows our human plight. And this One who possesses all power and authority in heaven desires and seeks what is best for us.

KING OF GLORY

Christian commentators on Scripture have long viewed Psalms 24:7–10 as a foreshadowing of Christ's ascension into heaven. He is the "King of glory," a victorious warrior prince returning from battle, to whom the gates of heaven must open.

In ancient times, kings and military generals returning victorious from battle sometimes entered a great city in a grand, glorious procession to exult and to receive the praises of their people. The parade through the jubilant crowds often included enemy rulers and generals who were humiliated by being led around in chains. The spoils of war were also on display, to be distributed to the people as gifts.

Paul uses this imagery to speak of Christ's ascension to heaven in triumphant glory. Echoing words from Psalm 68:18, he declares that "when he ascended on high he led a host of captives, and he gave gifts to men" (Eph 4:8). Similar imagery appears in his letter to the Colossians: "[Christ] disarmed the principalities and powers and made a public example of them, triumphing over them" (Col 2:15). The "captives" are the demonic powers that have oppressed God's people; "principalities and powers" refers to hierarchical ranks among the demons. The "gifts" are the graces Christ bestows on the Church through the Holy Spirit.

Even so, the King's conquest of his demonic enemies

isn't the only royal victory to be celebrated. The men who are driven by those dark powers to destroy the King's people on earth must also be vanquished. Turning to the book of Revelation, we find that glorious triumph portrayed.

THE KING IN THE BOOK OF REVELATION

Imagine the dilemma of the earliest Christians. They know the truth about Jesus, as Paul and others have preached to them: He is the Christ, sent by God to care for his people, die for them, and rise again. He has ascended into heaven, far beyond their sight.

If they are to see him now, it must be with the eyes of faith. But with their bodily eyes, they see themselves surrounded by those who hate them for their faith. The Jewish religious authorities seek their expulsion. The Roman imperial forces hunt them down brutally to torture and murder them. The Emperor Nero has even crucified Christians and burned them alive to use as human torches for his garden parties.

What would it mean to these anguished souls to know that Jesus is the King of kings?

Our Lord's victory and his reign in heaven must at times seem to them remote during these persecutions of the Church. The power of Rome appears invincible, and the empire's hatred for Christ and his followers appears implacable. The political powers conspire to crush them utterly and without mercy. Is there any hope for the infant Church?

In writing the book of Revelation around the end of the first century, St. John answers that question with a thunderous *yes!* Jesus Christ—who died, rose again, and ascended into heaven—is himself their great hope! This is the overarching theme of the book. John reports his inspiring, consoling vision of their Lord enthroned with God the Father, and his prophecy of a glorious future for the holy ones who love him.

John's great desire, at the prompting of the Holy Spirit, is to reassure his Christian brothers and sisters that even if they cannot see Christ, his power and authority are absolute. In the end, not just the Roman Empire, but every other empire, will fall before him.

Nowhere is this intention for writing more clear than in John's descriptions of Jesus as a Warrior-King. In chapter 17, for example, he reports the words of the angel about the fate of those who "make war on the Lamb," Jesus Christ: "The Lamb will conquer them, for he is Lord of lords and King of kings, and those with him are called and chosen and faithful" (Rv 17:14).

Listen to the visionary's breathtaking description of our Lord leading the armies of heaven:

> Then I saw heaven opened, and behold, a white horse. He who sat upon it is called Faithful and True, and in righteousness he judges and makes war. His eyes are like a flame of fire, and on his head are many diadems. . . . He is clothed in a robe dipped in blood, and the name by which he is called is The Word of God. And the armies of heaven, wearing fine linen, white and pure, followed him on white horses. From his mouth issues a sharp sword with which to strike the nations, and he will rule them with a rod of iron; he will tread the wine press of the fury of the wrath of God the Almighty. On his robe and on his thigh

he has a name inscribed, "King of kings and Lord of lords." (Rv 19:11–16)

And what about John's terrifying portrayal of Jesus as Judge, one of his proper roles as King? John writes:

> Then I saw a great white throne and him who sat upon it; from his presence, earth and sky fled away, and no place was found for them. And I saw the dead, great and small, standing before the throne, and books were opened. Also another book was opened, which is the book of life. And the dead were judged by what was written in the books, by what they had done. . . . And if any one's name was not found written in the book of life, he was thrown into the lake of fire. (Rv 20:11–12, 15)

OUR KING, WARRIOR, AND JUDGE

Perhaps for many of us today, as we live in relative safety and comfort, these words seem chilling, even distasteful. We prefer democracies and republics to kingdoms. Worse yet, this Jesus is a fierce, blood-bathed Warrior-King. He strikes down nations and crushes them like grapes for making wine. With fire and a sword, he visits the wrath of God upon the world.

Doesn't Scripture call Jesus "the Prince of Peace" (Is 9:6)? How can this possibly be the same Christ?

Yes, these portrayals of Jesus may strike many of our contemporaries as alien, harsh, brutal. But for the earliest Christians, who suffered such horrific injustice at the hands of evil and powerful men—men who styled themselves great kings and lords—these words bring comfort and hope. John writes as well of those Christian martyrs of his day, those who have been hunted down and tortured and gruesomely murdered. He says he hears them crying out from heaven for God to bring justice to the earth.

In the end, John tells them, Jesus Christ is the King of those evil kings and the Lord of those wicked lords. They must submit to his divine power. At the coming of his universal kingdom, their reign will collapse. When his sovereign lordship is revealed, their power will be shattered. In the end, he will set the world aright; he will vanquish evil; he will judge all people in justice; he will rule all things in peace.

The common notion of Jesus as simply a sweet, mild-mannered man urging everyone to be nice fails to take into consideration such biblical passages that portray him as a fierce King, Warrior, and Judge. Yet the full scriptural witness to our Lord's identity and mission must be allowed to speak to us so that our portrait of him will not be seriously distorted by omissions that make us more comfortable—for now.

Should we interpret such passages as outdated excesses of a more brutish time and culture? We might as well ask: Is Jesus himself outdated and brutish? For in the Gospels, Jesus himself speaks of his role as judge in terms hardly less sobering.

Referring to himself as "the King," he warns that in the final judgment of the human race, he will command those who failed to love their neighbors: "'Depart from me, you cursed, into the eternal fire prepared for the devil and his angels.' . . . And they will go away into eternal punishment" (Mt 25:41, 46).

DIVINE JUSTICE

In all these unsettling biblical statements, we see revealed an attribute of God that is praised throughout Scripture and must not be denied: his justice. We hear often of God's mercy, and so we should. But his justice is no less a divine attribute. Holiness is not possible without justice, nor is peace. And final justice requires that the Judge have the power to overcome the wicked and to banish and punish them if they refuse to repent.

The ancient Jewish people understood this reality. Psalm 96 cries out in jubilation over the prospect of God's rule and judgment of the world: "Say among the nations, 'The LORD reigns!' . . . he will judge the peoples with equity. Let the heavens be glad, and let the earth rejoice; let the sea roar, and all that fills it; let the field exult, and everything in it! Then shall all the trees of the wood sing for joy before the LORD, for he comes, for he comes to judge the earth. He will judge the world with righteousness, and the peoples with his truth!" (Ps 96:10–13).

The Church Fathers also understood this reality, and they emphasize that those who go to eternal punishment have brought it upon themselves. Commenting on Jesus's warning about his role as Judge at the end of history, St. John Chrysostom (c. 347–407) observes: "To the others [on his left], Christ says, 'Depart from me, you cursed.' He does not say they are cursed by the Father, for the Father had not laid a curse upon them—their own works did it. . . . 'I prepared the kingdom for you,' he says, 'but the fire I did not prepare for you—rather, I prepared it for the Devil and his angels. But you have cast yourselves into it. You have imputed it to your-selves'" (*Gospel of Matthew,* Homily 79.2).

The possibility of eternal damnation is terrifying. But some kinds of fear protect us. "Do not fear those who kill the body but cannot kill the soul," Jesus tells his disciples; "rather fear him who can destroy both soul and body in hell"—that is, the divine Judge (Mt 10:28).

The fear our Lord talks about here is not an unhealthy fear based on a false view of God. Rather, it is much like the fear of touching a red-hot ember, based on an accurate per-ception of the suffering caused by wrong and foolish actions. This healthy "fear of the Lord," the psalmist tells us, "is clean." Through his commands to act justly, we are "warned; in keep-ing them there is great reward" (Ps 19:9, 11).

We may be tempted to turn away from the portrait of Christ as Warrior, Judge, and King. But our aversion must be redirected instead toward the wretched evil that he must conquer, judge, and rule over in justice. And we ourselves must live our lives in such a way that, like the psalmist, we can welcome the Judge, the King of kings, when he comes.

SOMEONE INFINITELY GREATER

So far in this study, we have considered Jesus's claim to a unique status far beyond that of a mere teacher or prophet. He doesn't simply show the way or teach the truth or model the good life. He is himself "the way, and the truth, and the life" (Jn 14:6).

We have also looked at the biblical witness to Jesus's iden-tity and mission, one role at a time, in an order that reflects the way in which many of his contemporaries would have grown in their understanding of him: first, through his ministry, as the promised royal Messiah; then, through his passion and death, as the sacrificial Lamb of God; next, through his resurrection, as the Victor over death; and then, through his ascension, as the exalted King of kings in heaven, "the Lord of glory" (Jas 2:1; 1 Cor 2:8).

In a sense, however, we have only begun to explore our Lord's identity and mission. As marvelous as the work of the Messiah turned out to be, in many of the passages we have studied we find hints that Jesus is Someone infinitely greater. In fact, a mere man—even one chosen and sent by God as Messiah—could not die to bring sinners forgiveness, or vanquish death by his resurrection, or ascend to the throne of the universe, as Jesus did. In our next chapter, we will see that despite appearances, the One who did all these things did not begin his existence in his mother's womb.

Scripture Passages to Ponder

Matthew 25:31–46; 28:16–20; Acts 7:54–60; Ephesians 1:15–23; Psalms 24:7–10; Revelation 17:13–14; 19:11–16; 20:11–15

> *All hail the power of Jesus' name!*
> *Let angels prostrate fall;*
> *Bring forth the royal diadem*
> *And crown him Lord of all!*
> *Let every kindred, every tribe*
> *On this terrestrial ball*
> *To him all majesty ascribe,*
> *And crown him Lord of all!*

FROM EDWARD PERONETT, "ALL HAIL
THE POWER OF JESUS' NAME!"

6

WORD OF GOD

*In the beginning was the Word, and the Word
was with God, and the Word was God.*

JOHN 1:1

The four Gospels all tell the story of our Lord's life. But they differ in how they begin that story. Matthew starts with Jesus's ancestry. Mark begins in Jesus's adulthood. Luke opens with the events leading up to Jesus's birth.

John, however, starts his Gospel long, long before these historical events—in fact, long before history itself is born. To tell the full story of Jesus's identity and mission, he must begin "in the beginning," before the very creation of the world.

The biblical book of Genesis tells us that God spoke the universe into being. The Gospel of John tells us that Jesus Christ is himself that eternal Word of God. He did not begin his life when he was conceived in his mother's womb.

IN THE BEGINNING

John's Gospel was written after the other three biblical Gospels, about the year AD 100. He often provides information about Jesus's life not appearing in the other three Gospels, supplementing what has already been recorded. He also is concerned to provide a more complete picture of Jesus's identity and mission, now that he and the other early Christians have had more time to reflect on what God has revealed to them through Jesus's life, death, and resurrection, and the events that followed.

This wider angle of vision is apparent from the very first words of John's Gospel. Rather than beginning his account with a human genealogy of Christ or historical events related to his life, John provides what might be considered a "divine" genealogy revealing our Lord's ultimate origins before history ever began. Echoing the opening words of the creation account in the book of Genesis (Gn 1:1), John announces, "In the beginning . . ." (Jn 1:1).

St. Hilary of Poitiers (d. 468) marvels at the visionary breadth revealed by John, who was only a humble fisherman when Jesus called him:

> Consider and decide whether it were the greater feat [of Christ] to raise the dead or to impart to an untrained mind the knowledge of mysteries so deep as he reveals by saying, "In the beginning was the Word." What does this "in the beginning was" mean? He ranges backward over the expanses of time, centuries are left behind, and ages disappear. . . . This fisherman of mine, unlettered and unread, is untrammeled by

time, undaunted by its immensity; he pierces beyond the beginning. (*On the Trinity,* 2.13)

The lines that follow offer a magnificent hymn that sings of Jesus Christ. John himself may have composed this hymn as he wrote his Gospel, or he may have based it on a hymn from a liturgy of the earliest Christians. (Early hymns seem to have been incorporated into other New Testament books as well: see Phil 2:5–11; Col 1:15–20; 1 Tm 3:16; and 2 Tm 2:11–13.)

"In the beginning," John continues, "was the Word, and the Word was with God, and the Word was God; he was in the beginning with God" (Jn 1:1–2). But who exactly is "the Word"?

THE LOGOS

The New Testament Greek term for "word" is *logos,* from which we derive the English term "logic" and a number of other terms as well. *Logos* can also mean "speech," "reason," or "plan," and in some ancient Greek philosophical circles, *the Logos* referred to the principle of reason or ordering at the core of the universe.

Under the influence of such Greek thinking, the first-century Jewish philosopher Philo of Alexandria (c. 15 BC to c. AD 45), an early contemporary of John, taught that *the Logos* was the intermediary between God and the universe, through whom the world was created and through whom human beings could know and understand God. Philo and other thinkers like him considered *the Logos* to be the transcendent mind of God, yet present throughout the universe.

In using the term *the Logos* to speak of Someone who was with God in the beginning, and was in fact God, John may very well have been building a bridge to the Greek pagan thinking of his day. But he was also drawing from the Jewish Old Testament tradition that spoke of God's "word" as his revelation of himself through creation, deeds of power and grace, and prophecy.

The psalmist proclaims: "By the word of the LORD the heavens were made, and all their hosts by the breath of his mouth. . . . Let all the earth fear the LORD, let all the inhabitants of the world stand in awe of him, for he spoke, and it came to be; he commanded, and it stood forth" (Ps 33:6, 8–9).

Another psalmist recalls from Israel's history: "He [God] sent forth his word, and healed them, and delivered them from destruction" (Ps 107:20).

The Wisdom of Solomon declares, speaking to God: "Your all-powerful word leaped from heaven, from the royal throne, into the midst of the land that was doomed" (Ws 18:15).

And the Lord himself speaks through the prophet Isaiah when he promises his people: "So shall my word be that goes forth from my mouth; it shall not return to me empty, but it shall accomplish that which I intend, and prosper in the thing for which I sent it" (Is 55:11).

The creation account in Genesis itself, though it does not use the phrase "word of God," nevertheless declares that the world comes into being when God speaks: "And God said, 'Let there be light'; and there was light" (Gn 1:3, with his creative speech repeated throughout the seven days of creation). We can easily see how, in light of this portrayal, later biblical texts would speak of God creating the world through his word.

THE WISDOM OF GOD

Some Old Testament passages speak of the *wisdom* of God in a similar way. It is his creative agent, which draws human beings to God and is identified with the word of God. "The LORD by wisdom founded the earth; by understanding he established the heavens; by his knowledge the deeps broke forth, and the clouds drop down the dew" (Prv 3:19–20).

Perhaps the most striking of such passages is found in Proverbs 8, where God's wisdom is personified (spoken of as a person) as Someone present "at the beginning of his work, the first of his acts of old" (Prv 8:22). Speaking in first person, Wisdom announces: "Ages ago I was set up, at the first, before the beginning of the earth. When there were no depths I was brought forth. . . . Before the mountains had been shaped, before the hills I was brought forth. . . . When he [God] established the heavens, I was there, when he drew a circle on the face of the deep, when he made firm the skies above" (Prv 8:23–25, 27–28).

Yet the Wisdom of God is not merely present at the creation of the world. Wisdom is also the agent of God's creative act: "When he marked out the foundations of the earth, then I was beside him, like a master workman" (Prv 8:29–30).

The ancient Roman Christian poet Prudentius (348–c. 413) beautifully merges the two concepts of divine Word and divine Wisdom. He writes that God's Wisdom has dwelt eternally within God's heart, and when uttered by him, was revealed as God's almighty, creative Word ("A Hymn for Christmas Day").

Given both the Jewish and the Gentile traditions about "the Word" and its parallel, "Wisdom," John seems to be

writing in such a way that both audiences will find an initial point of contact with his good news about Jesus. "In the
beginning was the Word . . . all things were made through
him, and without him was not anything made that was made.
In him was life, and the life was the light of men" (Jn 1:1, 3–4).

John affirms, as the Greeks believed, that the Word
(*Logos*) gives order and form to the universe. And he affirms,
as the Jews believed, that the Word reveals God, created the
world, and brings the life-giving knowledge of God to the
human race.

The fourth-century deacon and hymnist St. Ephraem
the Syrian (c. 306–c. 373) comments here: He "is called the
Word because those things that were hidden were revealed
through him, just as it is through a word that the hidden
things of the heart are made known" (*Commentary on Tatian's
Diatessaron,* 1.2).

A STARTLING ASSERTION

So John starts out in familiar territory with at least some of
his Jewish and Greek readers. But then he goes on to make
a startling assertion. The Word, "the true light that enlightens
every man, was coming into the world" (Jn 1:9).

Is God's revelation simply an enlightening message shining into the darkness of a sinful world? No—John goes on
to make a much more specific, and astounding, claim: "The
Word became flesh and dwelt among us, full of grace and
truth; we have beheld his glory" (Jn 1:14).

"The Word became flesh." The Word of God, John
declares—who existed before the creation of the world, and
through whom the world was created—the Word who was

with God in the beginning and was God, became a human being. The revelation, the manifestation, the creative power of God, was actually a Person, and that divine Person became a human Person. The Creator became part of his own creation.

But wouldn't such an unprecedented event have shaken the world? Wouldn't people everywhere have recognized the Word made flesh and living among them? Wouldn't they have acclaimed him as their maker and sovereign?

No, John tells us. "He was in the world, and the world was made through him, yet the world knew him not. He came to his own home, and his own people received him not" (Jn 1:10–11).

Such irony, and such tragedy. How could it be that his own creatures did not recognize or receive him? Were they blind? Or was he somehow hidden from their sight?

"The light shines in the darkness," John observes, "and the darkness has not overcome it" (Jn 1:5). The Greek word *katalambano,* translated here as "overcome," can also mean "comprehend" and is rendered that way in some other English translations. Similar English terms with such a double meaning would include "to grasp," which can mean either "to seize" or "to understand"; and "to master," which can mean either "to overcome" or "to gain a thorough understanding of."

Perhaps John intends both meanings: The darkness has no power to extinguish the light. In fact, the darkness is incapable of even recognizing and understanding the light.

Nevertheless, some of those to whom the Word came did receive him. They "beheld his glory" (Jn 1:14)—the radiance of his magnificence as the Word of God—and they responded in faith.

JESUS CHRIST, THE WORD MADE FLESH

Who was, in fact, this Word made flesh whom some came to recognize? John holds us in suspense until the seventeenth verse of the book, then he finally tells us: "Jesus Christ" (Jn 1:17).

The man welcomed by some as the Messiah—Jesus of Nazareth, the first-century Jewish man born to Mary in Bethlehem, executed at the order of the Roman governor Pontius Pilate, raised from the dead on the third day—is much more than just a man. He is more, even, than a man clothed with divine authority and power, fulfilling the exalted missions we have explored in previous chapters.

Jesus Christ is in fact the eternal Word of God, existing before the universe was created and instrumental in its creation. They are one and the same Person.

If we had not heard these words from John's Gospel all our lives, we would be dumbfounded by this assertion. Yet John, in his letters to the early Christians, insists again that this same Jesus with whom he had spent three years of his life as a disciple is none other than the eternal Word, who has brought life to the world: "That which was from the beginning, which we have heard, which we have seen with our eyes, which we have looked upon and touched with our hands, concerning the Word of life—the life was made manifest, and we saw it, and testify to it, and proclaim to you the eternal life which was with the Father and was made manifest to us . . . Jesus Christ" (1 Jn 1:1–3).

Nor is John the only apostle to make this electrifying claim. Writing decades before, the Apostle Paul declares of Christ: "He is the image of the invisible God, the first-born of all creation; for in him all things were created, in heaven and on earth, visible and invisible . . . all things were created through him and for him. He is before all things, and in him all things hold together. . . . For in him all the fullness of God was pleased to dwell" (Col 1:15–17, 19).

In another letter, Paul echoes the Old Testament references to the powerful, creative divine Wisdom, calling Christ "the Power of God and the Wisdom of God" (1 Cor 1:24). The author of Hebrews speaks of Christ in similar terms, as the one "through whom . . . he [God] created the ages. He reflects the glory of God and bears the very stamp of his nature, upholding the universe by his word of power" (Heb 1:2–3).

These stirring declarations teach us that Christ is not only the Creator. He is the One who gives the universe its coherence, its cohesiveness, its integrity; "in him all things hold together" (Col 1:17). He is the One "upholding the universe by his word of power" (Heb 1:3). Moment by moment, Jesus Christ keeps all creation from falling apart—from dissolving into nothingness!

If he does all these things, continually, is it any wonder, then, that he could walk on water, multiply food, heal the sick, raise the dead? We may marvel that the Word of God would deign to become one of us. But once we know that to be true, why should we marvel at any of his miracles?

Too often the canvas on which we try to paint our portrait of Jesus Christ is much too small. We need a canvas spreading out as wide as the heavens—and far beyond.

This Jesus, then, was much more than the promised Christ who was sent by God to establish an everlasting kingdom, to teach and forgive and perform miracles, to die as a sacrifice for the sins of the world, to rise again to conquer death, and to ascend into heaven to reign in glory. He did not begin his existence in his mother's womb in Nazareth. He had existed from before all time with God.

THE WORD'S RELATIONSHIP WITH GOD

Yet still we must ask: What exactly is the Word's relationship to God? Is he an active "part" of God? Is he an extension or a projection of God? Is he some kind of lesser god sent by the one, true, Almighty God proclaimed by the Jewish people? Is he a created being with power beyond all other created beings, through whom the others were made?

The answer lies, with simple brevity, in John's initial proclamation that this Word who was "*with* God" from the beginning "*was* God" himself (Jn 1:1, emphasis added). In the chapters to come, we must examine other biblical passages that will help us unpack that profound but mysterious statement.

SCRIPTURAL PASSAGES TO PONDER

John 1:1–18; Psalms 33:4–9; Genesis 1:1–5; Proverbs 8:22–31; 1 John 1:1–4; Colossians 1:15–19; Hebrews 1:1–4

> *Be thou my Wisdom and thou my true Word;*
> *I ever with thee, and thou with me, Lord;*
> *Thou my great Father, thine own may I be;*
> *Thou in me dwelling, and I one with thee.*
>
> FROM "BE THOU MY VISION"

7

I AM

Jesus said to them, "Truly, truly, I say to you, before Abraham was, I am."

JOHN 8:58

He calls himself "I AM" (Ex 3:14). From before all time, outside of all space, he alone is God: one, eternal, infinite, almighty, all-knowing, all-present, all-transcendent, all-good, all-holy, unchanging. He is the Creator of all things, the Sustainer of all things, the Lover of all things he has made.

He crafts the human race as sons and daughters who can love him in return. But they scorn him. He reaches out to them, again and again, calling them to return home to him: through prophets and priests, parted sea and fiery pillar, miracles of deliverance and catastrophes of chastisement. But again and again, they refuse.

So at last one night, he himself comes to them, born as one of them. He is "Emmanuel"—for the name means "God with us" (Mt 1:23).

This tiny Babe—his parents name him Jesus—grows up

and begins to bring heaven's life and light into the world. But even though he is God in the flesh, his humanity veils his divinity. Only on occasion does a beam of eternal glory break through, in his words or in his stunning works of divine power and mercy.

His mission is not to terrify those he encounters or overwhelm them with his glory. Instead, he woos them with his love and warns them with his truth. He heals and consoles and nourishes; he challenges and corrects and chastens. And in the end, he dies and rises again from the dead to open for them the way home.

ACCUSATIONS OF BLASPHEMY

In John's Gospel, we have seen, the evangelist declares that the Word of God made flesh, Jesus Christ, is God himself. John's account of Jesus's life and ministry then proceeds to illustrate this truth in various ways, as difficult as it might be for his contemporaries to accept. John shows how divine wisdom and power flow from this Man as from no other.

Most importantly, John reports how Jesus himself makes the claim to be divine. He announces himself to be not just a revelation of God, or a lesser god come down from heaven, but rather the one true God, the almighty Creator, worshipped by the Jewish people for generations, ever since their beginning as a distinct people sprung from their forefather Abraham.

Not surprisingly, such a claim scandalizes Jesus's audience, who accuse him of blasphemy—showing contempt or irreverence for God. And blasphemy it is indeed if the man making the claim is in fact only human. Yet if, on the other hand, he is telling the truth—if he is indeed both God and Man—then what may seem to be blasphemy or even fantasy is actually a matter of integrity and sanity. And if it is true, a great deal about all his other names and titles comes into clearer focus, and they are found to display a new, profound, and powerful dimension.

JESUS'S ENEMIES ARE SCANDALIZED

Jesus has adversaries aplenty, those who simply cannot believe that God could, or would, become a Man. We must not judge them too harshly, at least for their skepticism. The ancient Jews are passionate about keeping the name of God holy, as required by the second of the Ten Commandments.

For a man to take the name of God for himself, to claim that he is God, is for them a crime punishable by death. So serious is this offense that the ancient Law of Moses followed by the Jews prescribes death by stoning for the crime of blasphemy (Lv 24:16).

The Gospels report several occasions when Jesus is accused of blasphemy. Luke tells us how one day, Jesus speaks to a paralytic man he is about to heal miraculously. He says, "Man, your sins are forgiven you." But his adversaries challenge that statement: "Who is this that speaks blasphemies? Who can forgive sins but God only?" (Lk 5:20–21).

Human beings can of course forgive the sins committed against them by others, and they are commanded by God to do so. But Jesus is claiming to forgive in general the sins of someone he has apparently never met, who has never wronged him personally. Such offenses are ultimately against God (see Ps 51:4), and so God must be the one who forgives them.

Jesus makes no effort to challenge their reasoning. He

obviously agrees that only God can forgive in that way. But he responds to his adversaries' concerns by working the healing miracle as they watch, implying that he is in fact the God who both heals and forgives (see Lk 5:22–36).

On another occasion, Jesus is debating his adversaries while speaking of his relationship to God as his Father. (More about this relationship in our next chapter.) He declares, "I and the Father are one" (Jn 10:30). No mere prophet or teacher, if he were sane, would ever make such a claim.

They pick up stones to stone him. Jesus asks which of his good works (he has performed many) has provoked their desire to kill him. They reply, "We stone you for no good work but for blasphemy, because you, being a man, make yourself God" (Jn 10:31–33).

"Before Abraham Was, I am"

If they should need even clearer evidence that Jesus claims to be God himself, they need only listen to a conversation with his enemies that has been prompted by a reference to Abraham (see Jn 8:33). This ancient figure, of course, is highly revered by the Jews as the father of their people and their faith. It was Abraham who, many centuries before, first heard the call of the one true God, though he was raised in a pagan culture worshipping many gods. Abraham responded in heroic faith and obedience (see Gn 12:1–9).

In this conversation, Jesus's enemies claim a special status as descendants of Abraham; they have Abraham as their "father" (Jn 8:33, 39). They insist that as Abraham's people, they find Jesus's teaching suspect.

Next, Jesus replies with the provocative statement: "Truly,

truly, I say to you, if any one keeps my word, he will never see death" (Jn 8:51). Compare this statement to the declaration of Jesus we have already studied in chapter 4: "Whoever lives and believes in me will never die" (Jn 11:26).

His adversaries are outraged. They conclude: "Now we know you have a demon. Abraham died, as did the prophets. . . . Are you greater than our father Abraham, who died? And the prophets died! Who do you claim to be?" (Jn 8:52–53).

Jesus continues to engage and challenge them. He finally tells them: "Your father Abraham rejoiced that he was to see my day; he saw it and was glad" (Jn 8:56). The implication is that Abraham saw Jesus either in a prophetic vision of the Messiah or by a special privilege from God after Abraham died.

"You are not yet fifty years old," they object, "and have you seen Abraham?" Then our Lord speaks in terms whose meaning is undeniable: "Truly, truly, I say to you, before Abraham was, I am" (Jn 8:58). They take up stones again to kill him, but Jesus leaves.

Jesus's use of the present tense instead of the past tense—saying, "before Abraham was, I *am*," instead of "I *was*"—implies that his own existence is eternal, not within time but outside of all time. That much in itself echoes the opening statement of John's Gospel, that Jesus is the Word who was "in the beginning with God" before the universe, both space and time, was even created (Jn 1:2).

THE DIVINE NAME

Even so, the implications of what Jesus says here are infinitely greater, and they are readily understood by his Jewish listeners. From childhood they would all have been familiar with an ancient biblical story in the book of Exodus, in which God appears to Moses at the burning bush on a mountain (Ex 3:1–15). There, the Lord identifies himself by saying, "I am the God of your father, the God of Abraham, the God of Isaac, and the God of Jacob" (v. 6).

As we learned in chapter 3, God gives Moses the mission of liberating his people, the Israelites (ancestors of the Jews), from slavery in Egypt (Ex 3:7–12). The people have been in bondage for four centuries, surrounded and oppressed by a pagan people worshipping other gods. Many of them, then, have forgotten, or perhaps never even heard of, the God of Abraham.

So Moses understandably asks the Lord: "If I come to the sons of Israel and say to them, 'The God of your fathers has sent me to you,' and they ask me, 'What is his name?' what shall I say to them?" (Ex 3:13). God replies to Moses, "I AM who I AM. . . . Say this to the sons of Israel: 'I AM has sent me to you'" (v. 14).

The Fathers of the Church pondered deeply this divine name. As the name that God has chosen for himself, they knew it must have profound meaning. St. Ambrose commented: "The Lord said, 'I am who I am.' . . . This is the true name of God: always to exist" (Letter 55.8:8).

St. Gregory of Nazianzus put it this way: "God always was and is and will be, or rather always 'is,' for 'was' and 'will be' belong to our divided time and transitory nature; but he is always 'he who is,' and he gave himself this name when he consulted with Moses on the mountain. For holding everything together in himself, he possesses being, neither beginning nor ending. He is like a kind of boundless and limitless sea of being, surpassing all thought and time and nature" (Oration 38.7).

Consider for a moment how Jesus's listeners would react when he calls himself "I AM." His adversaries are outraged, of course, but we can imagine that even his disciples are astonished. The pagan Greeks and Romans of their day speak of multiple gods with limited powers, sometimes taking on human appearances for a visit to the world of men. But the Jews know that the true God is not like that.

The true God is one; he is almighty; he is transcendent; he is eternal. How can this man Jesus be one and the same with such a God? Yet this is precisely what Jesus is claiming and what John is telling us to be the ultimate truth about Jesus's identity.

ALLUSIONS TO "I AM"

In several other passages in John's Gospel as well, Jesus alludes to this name of God in referring to himself. But the reference is typically hidden in English translation: Jesus says, "I am" (Greek *ego eimi*), but the translators have added the pronoun "he" so that it reads "I am he." Three occasions of this allusion are found in John 8:24, 13:19, and 18:1–6.

In the first, Jesus tells those who are rejecting him, "You will die in your sins unless you believe that *I am*" (Jn 8:24; there is no pronoun "he"; emphasis added). In the second, our Lord tells his Apostles that he will be betrayed, then adds, "I tell you this now, before it takes place, that when it does take place you may believe that *I am*" (13:19; again, there is no pronoun "he"; emphasis added).

The third occasion of this allusion to the divine "I am"

involves a remarkable incident in the Garden of Gethsemane when Jesus has been betrayed by Judas. When the soldiers come to arrest him, asking for Jesus of Nazareth, he responds, *"I am"* (Jn 18:5, emphasis added). Immediately, those who have come to take Jesus captive draw back and fall to the ground (v. 6). They seem to have been thrown down by the power of that divine name.

"With no other weapon," St. Augustine comments, "than his own solitary voice uttering the words 'I am,' he knocked down, repelled, and rendered helpless that great crowd, even with all their ferocious hatred and terror of arms. For God lay hidden in that human flesh, and Eternal Day was so obscured in his human limbs that he was looked for with lanterns and torches to be slain in the darkness. 'I am,' he says, and throws the wicked to the ground" (*Tractates on the Gospel of John,* 112.3).

Even so, immediately afterward, Jesus's enemies are able to stand up again, bind him, and take him away to his trial and execution. St. Augustine concludes in the same commentary that Jesus has demonstrated his divine power to prevent his own arrest momentarily, because his enemies need to know (as do we) that he is giving himself up willingly: "I lay down my life, that I may take it again. No one takes it from me, but I lay it down of my own accord. I have power to lay it down, and I have power to take it again" (Jn 10:17–18).

THE INCARNATE GOD

In addition to these more hidden biblical references to Jesus as God in the flesh, we find several others that are more direct. In describing the events leading up to our Lord's birth,

Matthew's Gospel (1:23) explains (referring to Is 7:14): "All this took place to fulfill what the Lord had spoken by the prophet: 'Behold, a virgin shall conceive and bear a son, and his name shall be called Emmanuel' (which means, God with us)." In a second passage, the prophet speaks of the Messiah to be born one day, and gives as one of his names "Almighty God" (Is 9:6).

This earth-shaking reality—that God has become Man in Jesus Christ—is known as the *Incarnation,* from the Latin term for "in flesh." It is one of two essential doctrines that stand at the heart of the Christian faith and set it apart from all other faiths. (The second of these doctrines will be considered in the next chapter.)

If God himself took flesh to become a Man—and who would dare say that God could not do just that if he chose?—how might that event deepen our understanding of the other names and titles we have examined in previous sessions?

Consider, for example, the other titles Jesus claims for himself in the Gospel of John with statements that begin: "I am . . ." "I am the way and the truth and the life" (Jn 14:6). If Jesus is God, then of course he himself is the way to God, the truth about God, the life of God! How else could it be?

Think of Jesus as the Messiah, the sovereign of a royal kingdom. If the King is God himself, then of course his reign will in the end extend to all nations and last forever. If the Lamb of God is not a sinful man with his own debt of sins to pay, but instead a perfectly innocent Man who is also the utterly holy and righteous God, then he can pay the debt of the entire human race in full. If the Man who has risen from the dead is also God, then he can certainly conquer death forever and offer us eternal life.

Yet the revelation that Jesus Christ is God himself leaves us with pressing questions: When Jesus prays to the Father in heaven, is he somehow just talking to himself? Are "Father" and "Son" just two names to designate two roles taken on by the one God? Or perhaps there are actually two Gods? Early Christians found themselves wrestling with these critical issues, which our next chapter will address.

COUNTERFEIT, CRAZY, OR CREATOR?

Given these claims that Jesus makes for himself, whatever else we may say about him, we cannot claim that he is just a good man. If he is only a man, and not also God, then he is not good at all. Clearly claiming to be God, on this and other occasions, he is either a lying counterfeit or a raving madman.

On the other hand, if Jesus is who he says he is, then this reality demands a response. Every man, woman, and child is called to know him, to place their faith in him, to love him. If he truly is the great "I AM"—and he is—if he is our Creator who has loved us into existence, who is the very Source of our life, then we owe him our worship, our service, and our obedience as our Lord.

SCRIPTURAL PASSAGES TO PONDER

Luke 5:17–26; John 8:21–25, 39–43, 50–59; 10:30–34; 13:18–20; 18:1–6; Exodus 3:1–15; Isaiah 7:13–14; 9:6–7; Matthew 1:22–23

Before the hills in order stood
Or earth received her frame,
From everlasting thou art God

To endless years the same.
A thousand ages in thy sight
Are like an evening gone;
Short as the watch that ends the night
Before the rising sun.

FROM ISAAC WATTS, "O GOD,
OUR HELP IN AGES PAST"

8

SON OF GOD

*And a voice came from heaven, "You are my
beloved Son; with you I am well pleased."*

LUKE 3:22

The Old Testament book of Deuteronomy declares, "The
LORD our God is one LORD" (Dt 6:4). Surrounded by peoples
worshipping multiple gods, the ancient Israelites needed that
reminder: There is only one true God.

In the New Testament, John's first epistle tells us about
this one God, "God is love" (1 Jn 4:8). This simple statement
has profound implications. Note that John doesn't say just that
God loves, but that God *is* love; in himself, *he is love.* He did
not begin to love when he created a universe to love. In his
unchanging nature, he is love from before all time.

But how could this be if God is one? Love is a relationship
between persons, between someone who loves and someone
who is loved. Before God brought time and space into being,
how could God be love if he is solitary?

The answer: God is one, but he is by no means solitary.

God is love because a relationship of love exists within God himself.

A Communion of Persons

The Church teaches us that God is a communion of Persons, the Lover and the Beloved. From all eternity, the Father loves the Son, and the Son loves the Father. And the Love between them is himself a Person, the Holy Spirit. The *Catechism of the Catholic Church* puts it this way: "St. John goes even further when he affirms that 'God is love' [1 Jn 4:8, 16]: God's very being is love. By sending his only Son and the Spirit of Love in the fullness of time, God has revealed his innermost secret: God himself is an eternal exchange of love, Father, Son and Holy Spirit, and he has destined us to share in that exchange [1 Cor 2:7–16; Eph 3:9–12]" (CCC 221).

At the heart of the Christian faith stands this revelation of God about himself. It is fundamental to understanding the identity and mission of Jesus Christ. In the previous chapter, we noted that the Incarnation is an essential truth affirmed by the Christian faith that sets it apart from all other faiths. The Triune ("Three-in-One") nature of God is another such truth.

Knowing that this Blessed Trinity is a reality allows us to say that "God is love." And we can affirm that out of the superabundance of this love, flowing eternally among the Father, Son, and Holy Spirit, God created the world.

We catch glimpses of this innermost secret of the divine nature by looking closely at the life of Jesus Christ. For he is the Second Person of that Blessed Trinity, God the Son, who entered the world by taking on our human nature so that we could enter into that eternal life of love.

GOD THE FATHER

When Jesus teaches his disciples, he repeatedly refers to God as their "heavenly Father" and instructs them to call God "Father" in prayer. This designation would not be unfamiliar to Jesus's Jewish audience. In a number of Old Testament passages, God is called the "father" of the nation of Israel as a whole.

Toward the end of his life, for example, Moses says to the people assembled: "Is not he [God] your father, who created you, who made you and established you?" (Dt 32:6). Such language is echoed later by the prophets Isaiah (63:16; 64:8), Jeremiah (3:4, 19), and Malachi (1:6; 2:10). It can also be found in Tobit (13:4) and the Old Testament wisdom literature (Ws 14:3; Sir 23:1, 4). Still other Old Testament passages allude to God's fatherhood without actually calling him father (Ex 4:22–23; Dt 1:31; 8:5; 14:1; Ps 103:13; Jer 3:22; 31:20; Hos 11:1–4; Mal 3:17).

Occasionally in the Old Testament, God is called the father of individuals, especially the king (2 Sm 7:14; 1 Chr 7:13; 22:10; 28:6; Ps 2:7–8; 89:6). But he is also known as the father of the fatherless (Ps 68:5) and the afflicted (Sir 51:10).

One of these Old Testament passages, especially memorable, is found in the Wisdom of Solomon. In it, we hear the plotting of wicked men against a righteous man who claims God as his Father. It is a foreshadowing of Jesus's passion and death:

> Let us lie in wait for the righteous man, because he is inconvenient to us and opposes our actions. . . . He professes to have knowledge of God, . . . and boasts that God is his father. Let us see if these words are

true, and let us test what will happen at the end of his life; for if the righteous man is God's son, he will help him and deliver him from the hand of his adversaries. Let us test him with insult and torture. . . . Let us condemn him to a shameful death. (Ws 2:12–13, 16–20)

Compare this description with Matthew's account of our Lord's crucifixion centuries later, especially the words of his enemies who mocked him as he hung on the Cross: "'If you are the Son of God, come down from the cross.' . . . 'He trusts in God; let God deliver him now, if he desires him; for he said, "I am the Son of God"'" (Mt 27:40, 43).

The parallels are striking. Even so, the mockery at Calvary suggests that Jesus's adversaries recognize that his claim to be the Son of God goes well beyond the kind of claims for God's fatherhood familiar to them from the Old Testament Scriptures. What would lead them to that conclusion?

JESUS'S UNIQUE STATUS AS SON

Though only these few references to God as a father appear in the Old Testament, Jesus gives that name precedence over all others. In the first three Gospels, he is recorded using it sixty-five times, and in the Gospel of John, more than a hundred times. If we examine more closely Jesus's relationship to God as the New Testament portrays it, we discover that he is the Son of the heavenly Father in a way unlike any other man.

His unique divine Sonship is announced even before his birth. We saw in chapter 2 how the Archangel Gabriel's message to Mary, reported by Luke, about the Child she will conceive makes it clear that he will be the Messiah, destined to rule on "the throne of his father [that is, his forefather]

David" (Lk 1:32). But the more astonishing announcement of the angel, of course, is that the Child will be conceived without a human father.

We know little about Jesus's childhood and youth. But the well-known incident in Jerusalem when he is twelve years old, also reported in the Gospel of Luke, shows clearly his awareness that God is his Father in a way that Joseph is not.

Having lost track of Jesus, Mary and Joseph search until they discover him with the teachers in the Temple, the house of God. When Mary tells him how anxious they have been in their search, he replies: "Did you not know that I must be in my Father's house?" (Lk 2:49).

Many years later, when the time comes for Jesus to begin his public ministry, God himself claims Jesus as his Son in a way that is utterly unprecedented. When John the Baptist is baptizing our Lord at his request, the Holy Spirit descends on him in the form of a dove, and a voice comes from heaven: "You are my beloved Son; with you I am well pleased" (Lk 3:22). The Father calls Jesus, not just his Son, but his beloved Son, a divine testimony to that eternal love within the Trinity.

The Father's voice comes thundering again at a crucial point in Jesus's public ministry. One day he is transfigured in brilliant light upon the mountaintop while the Apostles Peter, James, and John are watching. God speaks again from heaven, saying, "This is my beloved Son, with whom I am well pleased; listen to him" (Mt 17:1–8). The event makes such an impression on Peter that it will later be recalled in one of his letters, noting how the words of God the Father bestowed honor and glory on his Son (2 Pt 1:16–18).

INTIMACY WITH THE FATHER

This loving relationship of Father and Son shines throughout Jesus's ministry. The Gospel of John portrays it most clearly. In his very first chapter, John tells us that the Word who was with God in the beginning, who "became flesh and dwelt among us" (whom we encountered in chapter 6) was also "the only-begotten Son from the Father," who "is in the bosom of the Father" (Jn 1:14)—an image that conveys the deepest intimacy and communion.

The Gospel of Matthew reveals an important dimension of this intimacy when Jesus speaks of the mutual knowledge of the Father and the Son: "No one knows the Son except the Father, and no one knows the Father except the Son and any one to whom the Son chooses to reveal him" (Mt 11:27).

Another indicator of Jesus's intimacy with his heavenly Father is the affectionate title he uses when speaking to him. It is the Aramaic word *Abba*, used by children to speak familiarly to their fathers, much as English speakers might call their fathers "Papa" or even "Daddy." (Aramaic was the common language of the Jews of Jesus's day who lived in what is now Israel and Palestine; it is related to Hebrew.) The Gospel of Mark reports that Jesus uses this term of endearment for his Father when he cries out in agony in the Garden of Gethsemane, on the night of his betrayal and arrest (Mk 14:36). And in his final cry from the Cross, the Son commits his spirit, with complete trust, into his Father's hands.

The other Gospel writers usually translate *Abba* with the Greek term *Pater* (Father). But we know that at least some of the early Christians followed Jesus's example in calling God

Abba because the Apostle Paul uses the term in writing his letters (Gal 4:6; Rom 8:15).

Jesus's own words about his relationship with the Father express not only their intimacy but also his complete dependence on the Father and cooperation with the Father in all that he does. "Truly, truly, I say to you, the Son can do nothing of his own accord, but only what he sees the Father doing; for whatever he does, that the Son does likewise. For the Father loves the Son, and shows him all that he himself is doing" (Jn 5:19–20).

JESUS'S PRAYER IN GETHSEMANE

The Gospels tell us that Jesus often retreats to a secluded place to pray (for example, before he calls the Apostles; Lk 6:12–16). We have the high privilege of hearing the intimate words he speaks to his Father in the Garden of Gethsemane on the night he is betrayed—what has been called his high priestly prayer, interceding for his followers (Jn 17:1–26). This prayer offers us a number of insights into Jesus's mind and heart, but for now, we will focus on what it tells us about the divine Father-Son relationship.

First, Jesus speaks often of the glory he receives from the Father, even as he himself gives the Father glory (Jn 17:1, 4–5). They have shared this glory in heaven from before all time (v. 5). During Jesus's earthly ministry, one expression of this relationship is mutual recognition and honor: The Son has glorified the Father through his words and deeds; the Father has glorified the Son publicly at his baptism and transfiguration, and will do so again through his resurrection and ascension.

Second, Jesus talks about the mutual sharing of the Father and Son. All that the Son has comes from the Father and belongs to the Father. All that the Father has is the Son's as well (Jn 17:7, 10; see also 16:15: "All that the Father has is mine").

Third, Jesus speaks of his oneness with the Father: The Son is in the Father, and the Father is in the Son (Jn 17:21). These words echo his previous public declaration, which so enraged his adversaries: "I and the Father are one" (10:30).

Finally, in this beautiful, powerful prayer, Jesus speaks of the mutual love of the Father and the Son, which includes all these relational aspects and much more (Jn 17:23–24, 26). The Father himself has spoken twice from heaven to affirm this love publically, at the Son's baptism and at his transfiguration. Both times, the Father calls Jesus "my beloved Son" (Lk 3:22; Mt 17:5).

The reality of God's own inner nature is beyond our full understanding. But the Church's teaching about it helps us to describe it in a way that takes into account the various truths about Christ's identity as we have encountered them in Scripture.

The eternal Word was *with* God (implying a distinction between them), yet the Word *was* God (implying their oneness). The Son prays to the Father (who is another Person), yet he can truthfully declare that he "and the Father are one." The eternal, almighty God who calls himself "I AM" has sent his Son into the world, and yet the Son can also claim for himself the eternal, almighty name "I AM."

ADOPTED SONS AND DAUGHTERS

John's Gospel emphasizes from the beginning that because the Father sent his Son into the world, we too can become sons and daughters of the Father: "To all who received him, who believed in his name, he gave power to become children of God" (Jn 1:12). Later, John tells us how Jesus prays that his disciples will have a share in the mutual love of the Father and the Son (17:23, 26).

Nevertheless, we must note that John speaks of Jesus as God's "*only*-begotten Son" (emphasis added), telling us that his kind of Sonship is unique (Jn 1:14). He is the Son of the Father by his divine nature, "born of the Father before all ages" (as attested by the Nicene Creed, often professed in the Mass).

Precisely because Christ is the Son of God in this profound sense, we are able to call God our "Father" in a way that would be otherwise impossible. Through this unique Son of God, we can become what the Apostle Paul calls "adopted" sons and daughters: "When the time had fully come, God sent forth his Son, born of a woman . . . so that we might receive adoption as sons. And because you are sons, God has sent the Spirit into our hearts, crying, 'Abba! Father!'" (Gal 4:4–6).

St. Hilary of Poitiers summarizes the reality this way: "Many of us are sons of God. But he [Jesus] is Son in another sense. He is the proper, true Son by nature, not by adoption . . . by birth, not by creation" (*On the Trinity,* 3:10).

The Apostle Paul elaborates on our relationship to God as his children in his letter to the Romans: "For all who are led by the Spirit of God are sons of God. . . . You have received the spirit of sonship. When we cry, 'Abba! Father!' it is the Spirit himself bearing witness with our spirit that we are children of

God, and if children then heirs, heirs of God and fellow heirs with Christ" (Rom 8:14–17).

What is it that we will inherit from God with Christ? Our inheritance is eternal life itself (Mt 19:29)—"an inheritance which is imperishable, undefiled, and unfading, kept in heaven" for us (1 Pt 1:4).

So how does this "adoption" into the family of God take place? It comes with the sacrament of Baptism, when we are "born anew" (or "born again"), "born of water and the Spirit" (Jn 3:3, 5). "For in Christ Jesus, you are all sons of God, through faith. For as many of you who were baptized into Christ have put on Christ" (Gal 3:26–27). We are now "members of the household of God" (Eph 2:19).

The Church's continuing astonishment at this unparalleled privilege is expressed in the words of the Sacred Liturgy introducing the Lord's Prayer: "At the Savior's command and formed by divine teaching, we *dare* to say, 'Our Father . . .'" (emphasis added).

As noted in the Catechism passage we cited, God has destined us to share in "an eternal exchange of love, [between] Father, Son and Holy Spirit" (CCC 221). John's words in his first epistle sum up this lively confidence we have in Christ: "See what love the Father has given us, that we should be called children of God; and so we are" (1 Jn 3:1). To become children of God in this way is to gain a share in the eternal, infinite love of the Father, the Son, and the Holy Spirit.

SCRIPTURAL PASSAGES TO PONDER

Wisdom 2:12–13, 16–20; Psalms 2:7–8; 103:13–18; Luke 3:21–22; Matthew 17:1-8; John 3:16–18; 5:17–23; 17:1–12, 20–26; Galatians 4:4–7; Romans 8:14–23; 1 John 3:1–3

Children of the heavenly King,
As we journey, sweetly sing,
Sing our Savior's worthy praise,
Glorious in his works and ways!
Fear not, brethren! Joyful stand
On the borders of your land.
Jesus Christ, your Father's Son,
Bids you undismayed go on.

FROM JOHN CENNICK, "CHILDREN OF THE HEAVENLY KING"

9

SON OF MAN

*For the Son of man came to
seek and to save the lost.*

LUKE 19:10

One night a little boy couldn't sleep for fear of the darkness. "I'm scared," he said. "I don't want to be by myself in the dark."

His father tried to comfort him. "Don't be afraid, Son. God is with you."

"I know *that*," said the boy. "But I want somebody with some *skin* on him!"

God has always been with us, ever since he created us. But he knew that we needed somebody with some *skin* on him. Someone with a familiar face and a comforting voice; someone who knew what it is like to be all alone in the dark. Best of all, someone whose hand could turn on the light.

And so, then, God put some skin on himself—and a whole lot more.

Jesus is that God-Man. And in the Gospels he speaks of

himself, not just as "the Son of God," but also as "the Son of man."

POETIC LANGUAGE

Biblical scholars have long debated the background of the title "Son of man." But it clearly has roots in the Old Testament Hebrew expression *ben-'adam,* "son of man," which appears more than a hundred times.

In most of these Old Testament references, the phrase is simply a poetic way of saying "human being." "What is man that you are mindful of him," asks the psalmist, "and the son of man that you care for him?" (Ps 8:4).

Ninety-three times in the book of Ezekiel, God addresses the prophet using this title: "And he [God] said to me, 'Son of man, stand upon your feet, and I will speak with you'" (Ez 2:1). Once in the book of Daniel, the prophet Daniel is similarly addressed by the angel Gabriel: "But he [Gabriel] said to me, 'Understand, O son of man, that the vision is for the time of the end'" (Dn 8:17). Used this way by God and the archangel, the title seems to be a way of reminding the one addressed of his humble status as a mere mortal.

Nevertheless, the phrase is used in another passage of Daniel to designate a character of exalted, rather than lowly, status: "Behold, with the clouds of heaven, there came one like a son of man," who was presented by God ("the Ancient of Days") with a universal and imperishable kingdom (Dn 7:13–14). Here, the intention of the expression seems to be that the figure has a human appearance: He looks "like" a son of man.

Who is this "one like a son of man"? Many Jewish

commentators teach that he symbolizes the Jewish people as a whole, who will ultimately enjoy the long-promised Messianic kingdom. Others, especially in later interpretations, consider him to be the Messiah himself. Still others insist that the passage has no Messianic references at all.

When Jesus uses the words "Son of man" to refer to himself, both these ancient scriptural contexts of the phrase take on profound significance for understanding his identity and mission.

JESUS AS "THE SON OF MAN"

Jesus uses the expression "son of man" often: eighty-one times are recorded in the Gospels. But unlike the Old Testament writers who speak of "*a* son of man," Jesus always speaks instead of "*the* Son of man," using the words as a title referring to a particular man—and that man is himself.

Some of Jesus's references to himself as "the Son of man" are in the context of his earthly ministry:

"The Son of man has authority on earth to forgive sins" (Mk 2:10). "The Son of man came eating and drinking" (Mt 11:19). "The Son of man has nowhere to lay his head" (Lk 9:58). "The Son of man came to seek and to save the lost" (Lk 19:10). "The Son of man is lord of the sabbath" (Lk 6:5).

At other times, Jesus refers to himself as the Son of man in speaking of his passion, death, and resurrection: "He charged them to tell no one what they had seen, until the Son of man should have risen from the dead" (Mk 9:9). "For the Son of man goes as it is written of him, but woe to that man by whom the Son of man is betrayed!" (14:21). "The Son of man will be delivered into the hands of men, and they will kill him; and when he is killed, after three days he will rise" (9:31). "The hour has come; the Son of man is betrayed into the hands of sinners" (14:41).

Yet a third category of Jesus's "Son of man" statements refers to his future return to earth in clouds of glory with sovereign power to rule and judge: "Whoever is ashamed of me and my words in this adulterous and sinful generation, of him will the Son of man also be ashamed when he comes in the glory of his Father with the holy angels" (Mk 8:38). "When the Son of man comes in all his glory, and all the angels with him, then he will sit down on his glorious throne" (Mt 25:21–32). "As the lightning flashes and lights up the sky from one side to the other, so will the Son of man be in his day" (Lk 17:24). "The Son of man will send his angels, and they will gather out of his kingdom all causes of sin and all evildoers, and throw them into the furnace of fire" (Mt 13:41–42).

"COMING WITH CLOUDS OF HEAVEN"

We hear perhaps the most striking of Jesus's statements in this third category when he is standing on trial before the Jewish religious authorities. We have noted in previous chapters how many of his adversaries were scandalized by his claims to be the Messiah (the Christ) and the Son of God. Now they are demanding that he reaffirm these claims in court to be used as evidence against him.

"Again the high priest asked him, 'Are you the Christ, the Son of the Blessed?' ["The Blessed" is a title for God.] And Jesus said, 'I am; and you will see the Son of man sitting at the right hand of Power ["Power" refers to God], and coming with clouds of heaven'" (Mk 14:61–62). (Note here as well that in identifying himself, Jesus begins with the divine name we noted in chapter 7: "I AM.")

Jesus's repeated claims to be "the Son of man" who comes in clouds of glory to rule the nations and judge the world demonstrate unmistakable parallels to the "one like a son of man" in Daniel's vision. However his contemporaries may have interpreted that Old Testament prophecy, Jesus is claiming it for himself.

The book of Acts provides additional support to this understanding of Jesus as the "one like a son of man" in Daniel. As we noted in chapter 5, when Stephen, the first Christian martyr, is about to be stoned to death, he gazes into heaven and sees "the glory of God, and Jesus standing at the right hand of God" (Acts 7:55).

Stephen cries out, "Behold, I see the heavens opened, and the Son of man standing at the right hand of God" (Acts 7:56). In Stephen's vision, Jesus is identified as "the Son of man" in clouds of glory at God's heavenly throne, much as he is described in Daniel's vision.

Finally, Jesus appears as "one like a son of man" in the book of Revelation, glorious and powerful. His portrait there clearly recalls the exalted ruler and judge in Daniel's vision (Rv 1:13).

TWO NATURES IN ONE PERSON

In light of all these references to "the Son of man," what does the title have to tell us about Jesus Christ? First, it tells us that Jesus is in fact a human being. Though he is truly God himself, he has taken upon himself our lowly estate. He is both Son of God and Son of man.

Listen to the Apostle Paul's lyrical description of this marvelous reality: "Christ Jesus, . . . though he was in the form of God, did not count equality with God a thing to be grasped, but emptied himself, taking the form of a servant, being born in the likeness of men" (Phil 2:5–7).

In the early centuries of the Church, various Christian thinkers labored to understand how such a thing could be. Is Jesus truly God, some asked, but not truly a man, only *appearing* to be human so he could communicate with us? They had a low view of the human body, so they found it difficult to believe that God himself would take on a body.

But the Church firmly rejected that notion. The Incarnation is a reality, not a fantasy. Jesus has a real human body and a real human soul.

Others speculated that Jesus is just a Man in whom God came to live in a unique way, or whom God adopted as his Son in a unique way. But that would mean he is only like one of the prophets of old, on whom the Spirit of God came so he could work miracles or speak prophecy.

No, the Church insisted. Jesus isn't just a Man in whom God dwells to an exceptional degree. Jesus himself is God.

Besides, Jesus isn't a *committee!* He isn't two persons, one divine and one human, coordinating their actions within himself. He is only *one Person,* the Son of God, with *two natures:* His original nature as God, and the nature he took on as Man.

Others suggested that perhaps Jesus Christ is *part* God and *part* man—something like a hybrid. But that isn't the case either, the Church concluded. He is fully God and fully Man. He lacks nothing of what it means to be truly human. He not only has some "skin" on him, like the little boy said; he has a complete human body, as well as a complete human soul, with both a human intellect and a human will.

Guided by the Holy Spirit, in time the Church clarified the matter this way: Jesus Christ is truly and fully God the Son, the Second Person of the eternal Blessed Trinity. He entered our world by taking our human nature and joining it to his own divine nature, making it truly his own. So Jesus Christ is both fully God and fully Man. In him, two natures (divine and human) are united in one divine Person.

CHRIST THE MEDIATOR

This means that God himself intimately knows our human condition, knows what it's like to live as we live. Having been made like us, he knows how it feels to be hungry (Lk 4:2), thirsty (Jn 4:7), and weary (Mk 6:31). He is acquainted with sorrow, grief, and pain (Is 53:3–5). He understands what it means to endure rejection, misunderstanding, even betrayal. He even knows what it means to be tempted (Lk 4:1–13).

In this light, the writer of Hebrews concludes: "Since then we have a great high priest who has passed through the heavens, Jesus, the Son of God, let us hold fast our confession. For we have not a high priest who is unable to sympathize with our weaknesses, but one who in every respect has been tempted as we are, yet without sinning" (Heb 4:14–15).

If the role of a priest is to represent God to human beings, and human beings to God, then Jesus is most perfectly suited for that mediating role between heaven and earth. "We have an advocate with the Father, Jesus Christ the righteous" (1 Jn 2:1).

When Jesus is calling Nathanael to become a disciple, he

speaks of himself as the Son of man in a way that beautifully portrays this mediation through an allusion to an Old Testament episode. As reported in Genesis, Abraham's grandson Jacob dreams of a ladder between heaven and earth, which angels are climbing up and down (Gn 28:10–17). When Jacob awakes, he declares that he is at "the gate of heaven" (v. 17).

Alluding to this event, Jesus says to Nathanael: "You will see heaven opened, and the angels of God ascending and descending upon the Son of man" (Jn 1:51). "The Son of man" is like a ladder, a bridge, between God and the human race, taking us to the gate of heaven. The Church Father St. Ambrose (c. 340–97) in fact concluded that in this dream, Jacob "foresaw Christ on earth" (*Jacob and the Happy Life*, 2.4.16).

HUMAN, YET WITHOUT SIN

The Son of man took on our humanity to *heal* our nature as well. He wanted to heal every aspect of who we are. To do that, he had to join to himself every aspect of who we are.

So Jesus was like us in *every* way, except one: *He had no sin* (Heb 4:15). He was born without original sin, and throughout his life he never sinned. He never said no to God.

Now someone might ask, "But isn't it part of human nature to sin? How can we say Jesus is fully human if he has never sinned?"

That's a common assumption, because we know that we ourselves sin and everyone around us does as well. It seems to be normal.

But we have to remember this: In the beginning, it was not that way. God created humans without sin, and his desire for them was to remain without sin. If they had remained without sin, they would have remained fully human in the way he created them to be.

Once they did sin, however, their human natures were corrupted, compromised, disordered. They had a great defect, because they had lost their original righteousness. The truth is that sin is *not* a part of human nature. Rather, it is contrary to our human nature as God intended it; it deforms our human nature. Our sins have diminished the human nature God intended us to have, leaving us with a deficit of love, knowledge, wisdom, strength, power, beauty, joy, and much more.

In a real sense, then, because of our sin, we are the ones who fail to be fully human. Jesus is the One who is fully human, not just with regard to human physical limitations, but with regard to human spiritual and moral capabilities. And because he is fully human, he can serve as our Model if we want to be fully human as well.

CHRIST, OUR REPRESENTATIVE

Even so, the Incarnation—God's becoming a man—provides us with much more than a model for becoming fully human. When the Son of God became a son of man, joining our nature to his, he became our representative in the great sacrifice offered for our redemption from sin. He could suffer the penalty of sin—death—on our behalf because he is one of us. And he could rise from the dead on our behalf as well, conquering death and the Devil as our representative.

"Man indeed brought death to himself and to the Son of man," St. Augustine notes. "But the Son of man, by dying and rising again, brought life to man" (Letter 140, *To Honoratus* 9).

For this reason, the Apostle Paul speaks of Jesus as a new "Adam," the first father and representative of the human race: "For as in Adam, all die, so also in Christ shall all be made alive. . . . 'The first man Adam became a living soul'; the last Adam became a life-giving spirit. . . . Just as we have borne the image of the man of dust, we shall also bear the image of the man of heaven" (1 Cor 15:22, 45, 49).

Adam was the firstborn of the "old" human race, but Jesus is the firstborn of the "new" human race. Human nature is recreated in him and through him: "If any one is in Christ, he is a new creation; the old has passed away, behold, the new has come" (2 Cor 5:17). Jesus himself declares this new creation in John's vision reported in Revelation: "Behold," he cries out, "I make all things new!" (Rv 21:5).

Still there is more. Our human nature, joined to Christ's divine nature, not only suffered sin's penalty of death and rose again to conquer death. Our human nature, joined to his divine nature, ascended into heaven and is now at God's right hand; Stephen saw "the Son of *man* standing at the right hand of God" (Acts 7:56, emphasis added). The One who now rules the universe is *one of us!*

"But God, who is rich in mercy, out of the great love with which he loved us, even when we were dead through our trespasses, made us alive together with Christ (by grace you have been saved), and raised us up with him, and made us sit with him in the heavenly places in Christ Jesus" (Eph 2:4–6). We are seated with him there because he is our representative, and we are in him.

"TO JUDGE THE LIVING
AND THE DEAD"

From this exalted place in heaven, Christ will return to judge the world. As Daniel's vision reports, the "one like a son of man," who comes in glory "with the clouds of heaven," appears when the heavenly court sits in judgment, and the books are opened (Dn 7:10–13).

Epiphanius the Latin, a bishop writing around the end of the late fifth century, comments on the final judgment scene that Jesus describes in Matthew 25, when the Son of man comes in his glory:

> How can he be the Son of man when he is God and will come to judge all nations? He is the Son of man because he came to earth as a man and was persecuted as a man. Therefore this person who they said was a man will raise all nations from the dead and judge every person according to his works. Every race on earth will see him, even those who rejected him and those who despised him as a man. . . .
>
> He, our Lord, who knows our thoughts, who foresees all human works and knows how to judge righteously, will separate them according to the merits of each person, as a shepherd separates the sheep from the goats. (*Interpretation of the Gospels* 38)

Why should God the Father bestow the role of humanity's judge on God the Son? Precisely because the Son of God is also the Son of man. The Father, Jesus explains, has given him "the authority to execute judgment, because he is the Son of man" (Jn 5:27). Paul preaches about Christ: "God . . .

has fixed a day on which he will judge the world in righteousness by a man whom he has appointed" (Acts 17:30–31).

Consider the Western legal tradition that someone on trial should be judged by a jury of his peers. In a sense, we might say that Jesus is perfectly fitted to be our Judge: not just because, as God, he is all-knowing and just, but also because he is one of our "peers," in the sense that he is also a human being who intimately knows our condition.

The Nicene Creed summarizes this reality, and the hope it offers each of us who long for the return of the Son of man: "He ascended into heaven and is seated at the right hand of the Father. He will come again in glory to judge the living and the dead, and his kingdom will have no end."

SCRIPTURAL PASSAGES TO PONDER

Daniel 7:9–10, 13–14; Mark 14:60–64; John 1:43–51; 5:25–29; 1 Corinthians 15:21–23, 45–49; Matthew 13:36–43; Acts 7:54–56; Philippians 2:5–11; Revelation 1:12–16; Hebrews 4:14–17

Where cross the crowded ways of life,
Where sound the cries of race and clan,
Above the noise of selfish strife
We hear thy voice, O Son of man!
From tender childhood's helplessness,
From woman's grief, man's burdened toil,
From famished souls, from sorrow's stress,
Thy heart has never known recoil.

FROM FRANK MASON NORTH, "WHERE CROSS THE CROWDED WAYS OF LIFE"

10

SAVIOR OF THE WORLD

We have seen and testify that the Father
has sent his Son as the Savior of the World.

I JOHN 4:14

Years ago, a popular bumper sticker proclaimed in bold letters: "JESUS SAVES."

A slightly different version of that sticker offered a whimsical response from some Jewish drivers. It said, also in bold letters: "JESUS SAVES. MOSES INVESTS."

Those bumper stickers illustrate in a humorous way an important truth: The word "save" can have more than one meaning. And if the people using the word in conversation don't come from the same spiritual background, the result can be confusion.

Christians agree that Jesus, as the Gospel of John says, is "the Savior of the world" (Jn 4:42). But what exactly do we mean by the word "salvation"? What are we saved from, and what are we saved for? To answer these questions, we must examine the scriptural context of God's promise to save his people.

SALVATION IN THE OLD TESTAMENT

The root of the Hebrew term for savior is *yasha'*—to open wide, to set free. So a "savior" is one who liberates, delivers, rescues, brings victory and safety. Occasionally a human liberator is meant by the term (2 Kgs 13:5), but most often, the title is given to God by the people of Israel as a deliverer from their enemies, both military and spiritual.

"The LORD is my rock, and my fortress, and my deliverer," King David sings, "my God, my rock, in whom I take refuge, my shield and the horn of my salvation . . . my savior" (2 Sm 22:2–3). He is thanking God "on the day when the LORD delivered him from the hand of all his enemies" (v. 1).

In this instance, for David the meaning of "salvation" is concrete: God has preserved his life from those who wanted to take it. Because horned animals are typically strong and aggressive, and they fight with their horns, the "horn" was for the ancients a symbol of power (Dt 33:17; Nm 23:22; 1 Kgs 22:11).

God is usually described as the "Savior" of the entire people of Israel. In their struggles to survive against their national enemies, God delivers them. "God, their Savior," sings the psalmist, is the One who did "great things in Egypt" to save them from bondage there (Ps 106:21).

Through the prophet Isaiah, God tells his people: "Fear not, for I have redeemed you; I have called you by name, you are mine. . . . For I am the LORD your God, the Holy One of Israel, your Savior. . . . I am the LORD, and besides me there is no savior" (Is 43:1, 3, 11).

In Isaiah's prophecies especially, the theme of God as Savior, and the salvation he brings, is prominent. One passage that speaks of a glorious future for God's people proclaims that the day will come when foreign peoples will come to Israel, walking by the light God has given his people, with reverence and bearing fine gifts—in particular, "gold and frankincense" (Is 60:6). The Gentiles will serve "the Holy One of Israel" (v. 14). At that time, God declares, "You shall know that I, the LORD your God, am your Savior" (v. 16).

"A SAVIOR, WHO IS CHRIST THE LORD!"

Given Christ's divine identity and redemptive mission, we should not be surprised that "Savior" is a title given to him from the very beginning of his life on earth. The Old Testament declarations that God saves his people foreshadow his coming to earth as a Man.

Even before Jesus's birth, certain members of his family come to realize that his arrival will somehow be an act of God's salvation for his people. In the Virgin Mary's *Magnificat,* her song of praise to God when she visits her cousin Elizabeth, she speaks of God as her "Savior" in light of the angel's announcement that she will bear the Son of God (Lk 1:47).

The prophecy of John the Baptist's father, Zechariah, describes the events about to take place in this way: "Blessed be the Lord God of Israel, for he has visited and redeemed his people, and has raised up a horn of salvation for us in the house of his servant David, as he spoke by the mouth of his holy prophets from of old, that we should be saved from our enemies, and from the hand of all who hate us" (Lk 1:68–71). Note how he echoes David's words in speaking of "a horn of salvation."

This Savior was promised by God to the nation of Israel. As the Apostle Paul will later emphasize when preaching to a Jewish audience, from among King David's descendants, "God has brought to Israel a Savior, Jesus, as he promised" (Acts 13:23).

Yet note that Jesus is called, not just the Savior of the Jews, but "the Savior of the *world*," "the Lamb of God who takes away the sin of the *world*" (1 Jn 4:14; Jn 1:29, emphasis added). The salvation God promised long before, through Isaiah, brings together all the peoples of the earth into God's kingdom. The wise men from the East who travel to see the Christ Child, bringing him gifts of gold, frankincense, and myrrh, are just the first of the Gentiles to seek out the Savior (Mt 2:10–12).

The universal offer of salvation in Christ is also demonstrated many years later when he speaks to the Samaritan woman at the well (Jn 4:1–42). The Samaritans and the Jews have a history of mutual hostility, and though the two peoples have common origins, they have gone their separate ways. The Jews have come to view the Samaritans as aliens rather than fellow members of God's family. Nevertheless, after Jesus spends time with the woman and her Samaritan neighbors, they come to believe that he "is indeed the Savior of the world," not just of the Jews (v. 42).

The universality of Christ's saving mission is repeated throughout the New Testament. In preaching to the Gentiles, the Apostle Paul emphasizes that Christ "is the Savior of *all* men"; "God our Savior . . . desires *all men* to be saved" (1 Tm 2:4; 4:10, emphasis added). John's Gospel tells us that "God so loved the *world* that he gave his only-begotten Son, that whoever believes in him should not perish but have everlasting life" (Jn 3:16, emphasis added). In Luke's Gospel, Jesus tells his Apostles that repentance and forgiveness of sins should be preached to *all nations*" (Lk 24:47, emphasis added).

SALVATION FROM SINS

On the night Jesus is born, Luke's Gospel tells us that angelic hosts fill the sky to announce with great joy: "To you is born this day in the city of David a Savior, who is Christ the Lord!" (Lk 2:11). Given the Messianic expectations at the time, we can imagine that at least some of those who will hear these words will interpret them to mean that the Messiah (Christ) has come as a military and political savior to liberate God's people from the hated Romans.

A more private announcement of an angel to Joseph, Mary's husband, tells us otherwise. Matthew's Gospel reports the words of this heavenly messenger: "Mary . . . will bear a Son, and you shall call his name *Jesus,* for he will save his people *from their sins*" (Mt 1:21, emphasis added). As we have already seen, the Messiah's kingdom is not to be a political kingdom, but rather a spiritual one. He will bring salvation not from soldiers but from sins.

Note the significance of the personal name "Jesus." What is the connection here between that name and the Child's saving mission? "Jesus" is an English version of the Hebrew name *Yeshua,* which has the same root as *yasha'* and means "God saves" or "God is salvation."

This truth is echoed again and again throughout the New Testament: "He appeared to take away sins" (1 Jn 3:5). "In him we have redemption through his blood, the forgiveness of our trespasses, according to the riches of his grace, which he lavished upon us" (Eph 1:7).

As we saw in chapter 3, through the sacrifice of the Passover Lamb, God delivered his people from slavery to the Egyptians and the death brought by the angel. Now, through "the Lamb of God who takes away the sin of the world" (Jn 1:29), he will deliver his people from slavery to *sin* and its penalty of eternal death.

The Apostle Paul speaks movingly of how we experience salvation from sin in this life through our Savior, Christ Jesus. We become "slaves of sin," he observes, and the "wages" of such slavery is death (Rom 6:5–23). But he rejoices that "the free gift of God is eternal life in Christ Jesus our Lord" (v. 23), who frees us from such bondage.

Paul cries out a familiar lament: "I am carnal, sold under sin. I do not understand my own actions. For I do not do what I want, but I do the very thing I hate. . . . For I delight in the law of God in my inmost self, but I see in my members another law at war with the law of my mind and making me captive to the law of sin which dwells in my members. Wretched man that I am! Who will deliver me from this body of death?" (Rom 7:14, 15, 22–24).

For the Apostle, the answer to that question is clear: "Thanks be to God, through Jesus Christ our Lord!" (Rom 7:25).

FORGIVENESS AND JUSTIFICATION

This freedom from sin comes about in at least two regards. First, we are saved from our sins through God's *forgiveness*—the cancellation of spiritual debts incurred by sin, the liberation of the heart bound by sin. The blood of Jesus is "poured out for many for the forgiveness of sins" (Mt 26:28). Such forgiveness reconciles us to the God against whom we have sinned.

Two New Testament Greek words usually translated in English as "forgive" illustrate this reality powerfully. One of them, *apoluo,* means literally "to set at liberty." It was used in a political context to describe releasing a prisoner. The other, *aphiemi,* means literally "to lay something aside, to let go of something." It was used in financial settings to speak of cancelling a debt.

Christ frees us from sins, then, in the sense that he cancels our debts and releases us from captivity through the forgiveness of God that comes to us through him. As Paul puts it: "He has delivered us from the dominion of darkness and transferred us to the kingdom of his beloved Son, in whom we have redemption, the forgiveness of sins" (Col 1:13–14).

Returning to the Apostle's words about being captive to sinful habits, we can see the second sense in which we are saved from our sins through Christ: In him, we receive the grace to break free of the patterns of sin in our lives that have kept us in bondage. We become "transformed by the renewal of [our] mind" (Rom 12:2). We learn to "walk by the Spirit" rather than gratifying "the desires of the flesh" (Gal 5:16).

St. Gregory of Nyssa (c. 330–c. 395), a fourth-century Father of the Church, writes beautifully of our need for this kind of Savior: "Sick, our nature begged to be healed; fallen, to be raised up; dead, to rise again. We had lost the possession of the good; it was necessary for it to be given back to us. Closed in the darkness, it was necessary to bring us the light; captives, we awaited a Savior; prisoners, help; slaves, a liberator. ...Didn't these things move God to descend to human nature and visit it, since humanity was in so miserable and unhappy a state?" (*Oratio catechetica*, PG 45, 48B).

Scripture speaks of this gracious gift from God through Christ as *justification*: our being made just, right, righteous. "Since all have sinned and fall short of the glory of God, *they are justified by his grace as a gift, through the redemption which is in Christ Jesus*" (Rom 3:21–24, emphasis added).

SAVED FOR GOD HIMSELF

Even so, the salvation offered to us in Christ involves much more than freedom from the bondage of sin in this life. We are saved *from* sin, not just in this life, but in the next, and *from* its terrifying consequence: hell, the "second death, the lake of fire" (Rv 20:14), an eternity estranged from God. But what are we saved *for*?

We are saved *for* God himself. The Savior came to reconcile us to God so that we might live in glorious friendship with him both now and in the life to come. "For Christ also died for sins once for all, the righteous for the unrighteous, *that he might bring us to God*" (1 Pt 3:18, emphasis added).

Recall Jesus's words to his disciples before his death, resurrection, and ascension: "When I go and prepare a place for you, I will come again and will take you to myself, that where I am, you may be also" (Jn 14:3).

Salvation, then, is not simply our escape from hell. Salvation in its fullness is eternal life with God and in God—a share of, a participation in, the life of the Father, the Son, and the Holy Spirit. As Peter says, God has "called us to his own glory and excellence," to "become partakers in the divine nature" (2 Pt 1:3–4).

"We shall be like him," John writes in his first letter, "for we shall see him as he is" (1 Jn 3:2). This is God's promise of the "Beatific Vision," the vision of perfect blessedness, perfect happiness and fulfillment in heaven, where we will at last see our Lord, Paul promises, "face to face" (1 Cor 13:12).

Nevertheless, to arrive at that glorious destiny in heaven, we must "strive . . . for the holiness without which no one will see the Lord" (Heb 12:14). We must "work out [our] salvation with fear and trembling" (Phil 2:12). For "everyone who thus hopes" to see God face to face "purifies himself as he is pure" (1 Jn 3:3).

Our salvation, then—our being made righteous with the ultimate goal of perfection—is an ongoing process that requires our faithful cooperation with God's grace in Christ. "And you," Paul teaches us, "who once were estranged and hostile in mind, doing evil deeds, he has now reconciled in his body of flesh by his death, in order to present you holy and blameless and irreproachable before him, *provided that you continue in the faith, stable and steadfast, not shifting from the hope of the gospel which you heard*" (Col 1:21–23, emphasis added).

Some Christian traditions view salvation as exclusively a past event that took place when Christians made a confession of faith in Jesus Christ as Savior and Lord. They are convinced that this act of believing in him, and declaring that belief, has "saved" them by guaranteeing them a place in heaven. No matter what they may do for the rest of their lives, they insist, they will never have to face the possibility of hell because of their sins.

The teaching of the Catholic Church helps us understand that salvation is actually a gift far beyond this—not just a guarantee of escape from hell. Jesus Christ came to give us much more than a kind of eternal fire insurance policy. According to the Catholic understanding of salvation, which is rooted in Scripture, we aren't just saved from hell. We're saved from the bondage of sin, the disorder of sin, and we're saved *for* eternal life with God.

A NEW CREATION

God created us in his own image and created us for him-self—for nothing less than to know, love, serve, and enjoy him, both now and forever. Through sin, however, we have rebelled against God and rejected his friendship. As a result, his likeness in us has been marred, and we've separated ourselves from him.

Because God loves us so much, he sent his Son, Jesus Christ, to save us from such a terrible fate. The life, death, and resurrection of Jesus offer us, through the forgiveness of our sins, escape from eternal punishment. But that's not all. Jesus also *reconciles us to God,* opening the door to a full restoration of our friendship with him.

In this way, Jesus begins the process of a complete renewal of God's likeness in us, a healing of the brokenness that comes from sin. So salvation isn't just a way to avoid hell, nor is it just a past event.

On the contrary: Salvation in its fullness is God's new creation. To save us, he remakes us in his likeness—a lifelong process requiring our cooperation—so that we can once again think and love as he thinks and loves. This process finds its completion only in heaven, where eternal life is enjoyed in perfect harmony with him.

Those who are joined there with God forever in the deepest possible communion of love will achieve their greatest destiny. They will fulfill their deepest longing. They will become what they were made to be.

A SHARE IN GOD'S NATURE

More than that, the Scripture tells us, we will actually partic-ipate in God's own nature—we will have a share in it. Here's what we read in the second letter of Peter: God's "divine power has granted to us all things that pertain to life and godliness"—the word "godliness" means "being like God"—"through the knowledge of him who called us to his own glory and excellence, by which he has granted to us his pre-cious and very great promises, that through these you may escape from the corruption that is in the world, and become *partakers of the divine nature,*" or as some translations put it, "so that you may *share* in the divine nature" (2 Pt 1:3–5, emphasis added).

As the image of God is restored in us, and as we grow deeper in faith, hope, and love, we become more and more like him. The process finds its culmination in heaven. Then, as John's first epistle tells us, "we will be like him" fully, because "we will see him as he is," face to face (1 Jn 3:2).

So what does it mean to have a share in God's own nature?

God is infinite and eternal. In heaven, we too will no longer be bound by time and space. God is all-powerful; we will have a share in his power. God is all-knowing; we will have a share in his knowledge. God is all-wise; we will have a share in his wisdom. God is all-good; we will have a share in his goodness.

Most importantly, God is love. We will be able to love as God loves, perfectly and without any shadow of selfishness.

Consider this analogy: A lump of iron, in itself, is cold and dark. That is its nature. But if you place it in the flames of a blazing furnace, and leave it there long enough, it undergoes a transformation.

In time, the lump of iron is so fully immersed in the fire that it comes to take on the characteristics of the fire. Instead of being cold, it burns. Instead of being dark, it glows. Not only is the iron in the fire, but the fire is now in the iron.

Has it ceased to be a lump of iron? No—not at all. It's still iron. But now it has become like the fire into which it was plunged.

In a similar way, our human nature, when joined intimately to God's own divine nature, will have infinite new possibilities. And *that* new, transformed, perfected, limitless life with God and in God is what we call *salvation*. Such is the glorious destiny offered to us by Jesus, the Savior of the world.

SCRIPTURAL PASSAGES TO PONDER

2 Samuel 22:1–7; Luke 1:67–75; 2:8–14; 1 John 3:1–3; 4:9–19; 2 Timothy 1:8–10; Titus 2:11–14; 3:3–7; 2 Peter 1:3–11; Isaiah 43:1–3; 60:1–3, 15–18; Revelation 7:9–12; 12:7–11

> *Beautiful Savior! Lord of all the nations!*
> *Son of God and Son of Man!*
> *Glory and honor, praise, adoration*
> *Now and forevermore be thine!*
>
> FROM "FAIREST LORD JESUS"

III

Portraits of Jesus: His Life in the Church

11

CORNERSTONE

Behold, I am laying in Zion for a founda-
tion a stone, a tested stone, a precious
cornerstone, of a sure foundation.

ISAIAH 28:16

In Georgia, rising up more than eight hundred feet above the
ground near the city of Atlanta, is a massive dome of colorful,
granite-like rock, more than five miles in circumference at its
base, weighing more than a trillion pounds.

They call it Stone Mountain. It has towered above the
landscape, standing alone, for millions of years. More amazing
still, it extends an estimated seven miles below the earth's sur-
face, stretching out to provide a subterranean foundation all
the way to the next state. Meanwhile, many species of plants
and animals call this great rock their home, nestled into its
crevices and flourishing in its little freshwater pools.

We might well think of Stone Mountain whenever we
read in the Bible that God is like a rock. He, too, stands
mighty, beautiful, and immovable. He towers above the world,

unchanging from age to age. He too is a sure foundation for us, and in him we find our refuge and our home.

GOD, THE ROCK

Moses, David, Isaiah, and others among the ancient Israelites speak of God as a rock. The image suggests weightiness, stability, immovability, durability, and firmness of purpose. In the celebrated "Song of Moses," for example, the ancient leader of the Israelites proclaims: "I will proclaim the name of the LORD. Ascribe greatness to our God! The Rock, his work is perfect, for all his ways are justice. A God of faithfulness and without iniquity, just and right is he" (Dt 32:3–4).

King David sings praise to God in similar terms: "I love you, O LORD, my strength. The LORD is my rock, and my fortress, and my deliverer, my God, my rock, in whom I take refuge" (Ps 18:1–2; see also Ps 31:1–5; 71:1–5).

The ancient Jews took great consolation in their God, the Rock. They needed him desperately, because their national history was like that of many nations since then: an unstable cycle of prosperity and disaster, glory and infamy, obedience to God's Law followed by disobedience and divine chastisement.

God was a firm defense to those who clung to him. But those who turned away from him found him to be a massive obstacle to their wicked plans, and in the end, their rebellion was crushed beneath his weighty judgments.

A TESTED AND PRECIOUS CORNERSTONE

In Old Testament prophecy, a more specific kind of rock or stone associated with God's firmness of purpose comes into view. In one poignant passage of Isaiah, the Lord rebukes the "scoffers who rule this people in Jerusalem" (Is 28:14). Identifying their sins, he warns that he will send a powerful enemy to chastise them, "an overwhelming scourge" (v. 18).

Nevertheless, God promises, the time will come when he will send a new leader to replace the rulers of Zion. ("Zion" is a poetic name for Jerusalem, from the name of the hill in that city on which the temple was built.) "Behold, I am laying in Zion for a foundation a stone, a tested stone, a precious cornerstone, of a sure foundation. . . . And I will make justice the line, and righteousness the plummet" (Is 28:16–17; see also 1 Pt 2:6).

In this way as well, the colored rock of Stone Mountain can recall for us God's words in Scripture. It has been quarried for generations, and countless cornerstones have been carved from its beautiful and enduring substance. So it provides a reminder that from the Lord, the mighty Rock, will come a solid and beautiful cornerstone that God himself has carved for his own purposes.

Traditionally, the *cornerstone* (or foundation stone) of a building is the first stone laid in a masonry foundation. A well-laid cornerstone is essential to the proper construction of a strong, well-structured building, because all the other foundational stones will be laid out in reference to this stone.

A "tested" cornerstone is perhaps one that has proven not to crumble under the stress of a heavy load. A "precious" cornerstone suggests that it is made, not of some common type of rock, but of something more rare and thus more valuable: perhaps jasper or sapphire, emerald or topaz. (The foundations of the city wall of the "New Jerusalem" in the book of Revelation are adorned with such precious stones; Rv 21:18–21.)

The "line and plummet" in Isaiah's prophecy refers to the plumb line, the mason's tool used to make sure that what is built is standing up straight. Unlike the unjust older structure that God tears down, the new one will have divine justice as the standard for its construction.

A REJECTED CORNERSTONE

In Psalm 118, we find another prophecy about a cornerstone being laid: "The stone which the builders rejected has become the cornerstone. This is the LORD's doing; it is marvelous in our eyes" (Ps 118:22–23).

Stones must have a particular size, shape, and composition to make them suitable for building. Otherwise, the builders reject them as useless. But appearances can be deceiving, and the builders themselves may lack competence in discernment.

In this case, the Lord has overruled the builders. The stone they rejected has become, not only one of the stones in an edifice, but the cornerstone, the most important stone of all.

THE CORNERSTONE OF THE CHURCH

The saving work of Jesus Christ did not end when he ascended into heaven. In a sense, it had only just begun. He established the Church to continue his work on earth, until the day when he returns in glory to judge the living and the dead.

To continue his ministry, the Church must maintain a vital relationship with her Founder, who is the divine Source of her life, strength, and permanence. To describe this essential relationship between Jesus and his Church, the Scripture speaks of him as the cornerstone of her foundation.

In the New Testament, the Old Testament references to God as the "Rock" and the prophecies of his laying a cornerstone converge in Christ. In one of his parables, our Lord alludes to himself as a "rock" on which the "wise man . . . built his house" (Mt 7:24–25). Rains, floods, and winds beat upon the house, yet it stands firm because of its solid foundation in Christ.

Those who reject him, however, are like the "foolish man who built his house upon the sand." Without Christ as a firm foundation, the house collapses in the storm (Mt 7:26–27).

When opposition to Jesus and his message intensifies, he reminds his adversaries of the rejected cornerstone prophesied by the psalmist (Ps 118:22–33), implying that he is that stone, whom they are rejecting (Mt 21:42–44). The spiritual architects of the nation are guaranteeing disaster by failing to recognize that the stone is precious and essential to the foundation being laid for a new house in which God's people can dwell.

THE STUMBLING STONE

The rock and stone imagery takes on a more ominous tone when Jesus warns his opponents that if they reject the stone, they will stumble over it and be broken; it will fall on them, and they will be crushed (Mt 21:44). In several other passages in the New Testament, our Lord and his gospel are described in similar terms as a "stumbling stone" or "stumbling block" or "a rock that will make them fall" (Rom 9:32; 1 Cor 1:23; Gal 5:11; 1 Pt 2:8).

Those who reject Christ will fall and injure themselves seriously. His truth is rock-hard reality. If we throw ourselves against it, the rock will remain unmoved, but we ourselves will be bruised and broken.

The preaching of the Apostles echoes our Lord's declarations. When Peter and John are brought before the council of religious leaders in Jerusalem after the Day of Pentecost, Peter addresses them boldly (Acts 4:8–12). The assembly includes the high priest and his family, who were instrumental in arranging for Jesus to be executed. Peter declares: "Jesus Christ of Nazareth, whom you crucified, whom God raised from the dead . . . is the stone which was rejected by you builders, but which has become the cornerstone. And there is salvation in no one else, for there is no other name under heaven given among men by which we must be saved" (Acts 4:10–12).

Peter's first letter takes up the same theme when he speaks of the Church that Jesus has established as "a spiritual house" built out of "living stones," his followers (1 Pt 2:4). He quotes the passage from Isaiah and declares that the "cornerstone chosen and precious" laid by God as a sure foundation for his people is Jesus Christ (v. 6).

Peter goes on to quote the passage in Psalm 118:22 that says "the very stone which the builders rejected has become the cornerstone" (1 Pt 2:6–7). Jesus was rejected as the Messiah and Son of God by his adversaries, but the Man they rejected and put to death is actually the new and precious cornerstone of God's new people, the Church. Both prophetic passages are fulfilled in Christ.

Finally, Peter alludes to one additional passage of Isaiah. In it, the prophet warns the people of Israel that in retribution for their sins, God will become "a stone of offense," "a rock of stumbling . . . and many shall stumble thereon; they shall fall and be broken" (Is 8:14–15). Again, he is echoing the words of Christ; those who have rejected the cornerstone will fall upon it and be broken.

A ROCK OF HOPE

Despite its threats of disaster, such a declaration is good news for the early Christians. They find themselves targeted for annihilation by many of their non-Christian neighbors, both Jewish and Gentile. Peter is reassuring them that despite such brutal opposition, the Church possesses a divine strength and permanence, which comes from having Christ himself as the cornerstone of her foundation. He is that original "living stone" from which the other "living stones" draw their life, and they are firmly established because they are laid out in reference to him.

In the end, those who try to destroy the edifice of the Church will themselves fall. Even though at times the Church may seem to be destined for demolition, Christ her corner-stone will remain unmoved, her sure foundation.

The Apostle Paul echoes such warnings, quoting the Old Testament prophecies, in Romans 9:32–33. Then, in his letter to the Ephesians, he too speaks of the Church as a building established on Christ, assuring us that the foundation is firm: "You are fellow citizens with the saints and members of the household of God, built upon the foundation of the Apostles and prophets, Christ Jesus himself being the cornerstone, in whom the whole structure is joined together and grows into a holy temple in the Lord, in whom you also are built into it for a dwelling place of God in the Spirit" (Eph 2:19–22).

Paul points out an important feature of this holy building of living stones: It is not just a home for God's people. It is a temple, a dwelling place of God himself. He lives within his people through his indwelling Holy Spirit, and that indwelling is made possible through Christ, the cornerstone.

A STONE OF RECONCILIATION

The Fathers of the Church see yet another spiritual reality portrayed by this cornerstone imagery: Christ's bringing together of estranged peoples. A cornerstone is laid at the place where two perpendicular walls are joined together. So the prophecy, concludes St. Cyril of Alexandria (c. 376–444), "asserts that it is a cornerstone because through faith, Israel and the Gentiles have been joined in a spiritual union. For on the corners of a building two walls always come together, and where they meet they are fused into one" (*Commentary on Isaiah*, 28:16).

St. Augustine views this prophesied joining of peoples as a reality that began even in our Lord's nativity: "To the [Jews], the infant at birth is shown as the chief cornerstone announced by the prophet. To the [Gentiles], he is manifested at the very outset of his career. He has already begun to weld together in himself the two walls originally set in different directions, bringing [Jewish] shepherds from Judea and [Gentile] magi from the East" (Sermon 199.1).

In these passages we have seen Jesus portrayed as the Rock or Cornerstone that supports his Church as its foundation; the One who protects his Church by his firmness and durability from those who would demolish it; the One who joins peoples together. But if we look farther, we find yet one

more fascinating rock image from the Old Testament applied
to Christ in the New Testament.

A LIFE-GIVING ROCK

One day when Moses was leading the Israelites through the
desert toward the land God had promised them, they could
find no water to drink at the place where they had camped.
They complained to Moses and demanded that he produce
water for them to drink. At God's command, Moses struck
a rock, and water came gushing out to quench the people's
thirst (Ex 17:1–6).

An old tradition of the Jewish rabbis maintains that this
same rock miraculously accompanied the Israelites on their
journey through the wilderness. The Apostle Paul seems to
refer to this tradition when he tells the Corinthians that the
Israelites "all drank the same supernatural [literally, "spiritual"] drink. For they drank from the supernatural [spiritual]
Rock which followed them, and the Rock was Christ" (1
Cor 10:1–4).

Here, then, we have yet another Old Testament foreshadowing of Christ in the image of a rock, but with a rather
different meaning. Instead of an allusion to his rock-like
qualities (firmness, strength, permanence, immovability), the
allusion is to the supernatural quality of an extraordinary
rock: When it is struck, it pours forth life-giving water.

Paul declares that Christ is the life-giving rock; he
quenches our spiritual thirst. Some of the Church Fathers
went even further to note a more specific parallel between
the rock and Christ: The rock was struck with a rod, and

life-giving water flowed out. On the cross, Christ was struck with a lance, and life-giving water and blood flowed out.

The Fathers saw the blood and water from Christ's side as a figure of the sacraments of Baptism (water) and the Eucharist (blood), which flow from the graces of our Lord's passion and death. In this light, the water flowing from the rock in the wilderness is itself a foreshadowing of these two sacraments, which are foundational for the Church.

In commenting on this passage, St. Ambrose speaks of the privilege we have in receiving Christ's precious Blood: "For them, water flowed from the rock. For you, blood flows from Christ. Water satisfied them for the hour. Blood satisfies you for eternity" (*The Mysteries*, 8.48).

THE LIVING STONE

When the eternal Rock who is God takes on flesh in Jesus Christ, we find that all these prophecies and foreshadowings become a new reality. Jesus displays all the rock-like qualities we have noted: weightiness, stability, immovability, durability, and firmness of purpose. For those who adhere to him, he provides a firm, enduring refuge and a firm foundation.

To his adversaries, however, he is the weighty, immovable stumbling block over which they fall. Ironically, the hardness of this Rock is at once a strength to his friends, and a peril to his enemies.

Given this reality, Peter's first epistle offers us a great sense of hope, as he invites us to be joined to Jesus Christ, the Cornerstone, by being firmly fixed in his Church. "Come to him," the Apostle beckons, "to that living stone, rejected by men, but in God's sight chosen and precious, and like living stones be yourselves built into a spiritual house. . . . You are a chosen race, a royal priesthood, a holy nation, God's own people, that you may declare the wondrous deeds of him who called you out of darkness into his marvelous light" (1 Pt 2:4–5, 9).

SCRIPTURAL PASSAGES TO PONDER

Deuteronomy 32:3–4; Isaiah 28:16; Psalms 18:1–3, 31–32, 46; 31:1–5; 71:1–5; 105:37–42; 118:22–23; Matthew 7:24–27; 21:42–44; 1 Peter 2:4–10; Acts 4:8–12; Romans 9:32–33; Ephesians 2:19–22; Exodus 17:1–6; 1 Corinthians 10:1–4

> Christ is made the sure foundation,
> Christ the head and cornerstone;
> Chosen of the Lord and precious,
> Binding all the Church in one;
> Holy Zion's help forever,
> And her confidence alone.

FROM "CHRIST IS MADE THE SURE FOUNDATION"

12

BRIDEGROOM

Behold the bridegroom! Come out to meet him.

MATTHEW 25:6

"One thing have I asked of the LORD," declares the psalmist; "that will I seek after; that I may dwell in the house of the LORD all the days of my life, to behold the beauty of the LORD" (Ps 27:4).

We often hear about God's power and wisdom, his justice and mercy, his love and his holiness. But how often do we consider the *beauty* of God?

Perhaps the notion of a beautiful God seems strange because we think of beauty strictly in terms of our senses: sight and sound. We know that God in himself is inaccessible to our senses directly in this life, so how could we speak of God's beauty?

The answer is found in the biblical portrait of Christ as the Bridegroom.

THE ESSENTIAL BEAUTY

What makes someone beautiful? Each culture has its own standards of beauty, and these often differ. The color of skin and texture of hair, the contours of the face, the form of the body all have their role to play. And in our day, the social and entertainment media in particular presume to dictate who will be admired as the "beautiful people," with the rest rejected, or at best, ignored.

Yet even though these features tend to receive the world's attention, such criteria for beauty are surely shallow—indeed, literally skin deep. Meanwhile, whatever body fashion may reign today, that fashion will change; and time itself will steal both youth and form and even life itself from the most physically attractive men and women among us.

What is it, then, that constitutes a deep, essential beauty, a beauty that never fades?

I remember how, some years ago, I was reading about the life of Mother Teresa, now St. Teresa of Calcutta. I was astonished by the goodness that I saw in her life: the selflessness, the charity, the courage and fortitude and wisdom.

One day as I was studying a photograph of her smiling face, I thought: *That's the most beautiful face I've ever seen.*

Now the world would have called her anything but beautiful. Her skin was weathered by years of labor, and filled with the wrinkles of old age. But there was a light shining in her face, an inner light that radiated through her outward appearance.

That light, of course, was holiness. Her face was lovely with the beauty of holiness.

Echoing an insight of St. Thomas Aquinas, Pope St. John

Paul II once wrote: "Beauty is the visible form of the good" (*Letter to Artists,* 3). For me, the face of St. Teresa clearly illustrates this truth. Beauty reveals to us goodness. Understood in this way, we can begin to understand what it means to speak of the beauty of God.

THE BEAUTY OF GOD

Now even at the level of the senses, we can say that the natural beauty of our world points to a certain beauty in God. The orderliness, the symmetry, the due proportion in creation all express those same qualities in the divine Mind that created them. And even the lovely radiance of color and light are suggestive of his glory. As the psalmist insists, "The heavens are telling the glory of God!" (Ps 19:1).

But beyond these visible tokens of God's loveliness, the eye of the soul can behold in him a far more exquisite beauty—the beauty of holiness, the beauty of goodness. He is the perfection of goodness, and so he is the perfection of beauty as well. This kind of beauty is essential, not superficial; it radiates from God's essence. And because God is unchanging, his beauty never passes away.

Sometimes I look at a beloved family member or friend, and my soul is pierced with a certain sweetness because of the goodness I see there: the innocence of my little grandchildren, sleeping; the selfless sacrifice of my wife as she cares for our family; the faithfulness of a close friend who stands beside me when days are dark. In all these loved ones, the beauty of character shines forth. And through them I catch a glimpse of the character of God himself, who is all-good, and all-beautiful.

We might conclude, then, that in this life, we are limited to seeing God's beauty only remotely, through intermediaries of some sort. At one time, that may have been true. But when God became a Man, all that changed. God now has a face; and that face is the beautiful face of Christ.

In him we see the majesty of perfect goodness shining out into a fallen world. In him we see the splendor of perfect holiness illuminating the darkness of the human race, which has lost is way.

A lively depiction of such beauty appears in the scriptural images of Christ as the Bridegroom. The Gospels refer to him this way. St. Paul's letters elaborate on the role, explaining that Christ is a Bridegroom because the Church is his Bride. And the book of Revelation describes the marriage supper of Christ and his bride, adorned for the wedding.

THE HUSBAND OF HIS PEOPLE

Beginning with their Exodus from Egypt, the ancient Israelites experienced as a people a cycle of seasons in their relationship with God. They tended to alternate between periods of faithfulness, when they served God and obeyed his life-giving commandments, and periods of faithlessness, when they worshipped false gods and lived immoral lives contrary to God's commandments. (Of course, the same might well be said of God's people in every era.) During their wayward times, the Lord warned them through the prophets that chastisement would be necessary to bring them back to faith and obedience.

One poignant image appearing in the Old Testament prophets describes this relationship as a kind of stormy marriage between God and his people. Though the Lord remains a faithful and loving husband, Israel proves itself an inconstant lover and adulterous wife.

The prophet Isaiah tells of a time when Israel's faithlessness has been so grievous, and the resulting divine chastisement so severe, that the nation seems like a barren and hopeless widow, whose husband is lost forever (54:4–8). The people have been conquered by Babylonian invaders and forced into exile. But God has not abandoned his people forever. He will restore them to nationhood as he calls them back to himself in mercy and hope. "You will forget the shame of your youth, and the reproach of your widowhood you will remember no more. For your Maker is your husband, the LORD of hosts is his name. For the LORD has called you like a wife forsaken and grieved in spirit, like a wife of youth when she is cast off, says your God" (Is 54:4–6).

The Lord sings a gracious, reconciling love song to his wayward wife: "For a brief moment I forsook you, but with great compassion I will gather you. In overflowing wrath for a moment I hid my face from you, but with everlasting mercy I will have compassion on you, says the LORD, your Redeemer" (Is 54:7–8).

"I WILL ESPOUSE YOU FOREVER"

The prophet Hosea uses similar language to speak of his contemporaries: "The land commits great harlotry by forsaking the LORD" (Hos 1:2). Hosea writes at a time when the nation is worshipping idols, whom he describes as "her lovers" (vv. 7, 10, 13). As a result, they are living immorally: "There is swearing, lying, killing, stealing, and committing adultery; they break all bounds, and murder follows murder" (4:2).

The Lord warns the nation through the prophet that disaster is approaching (see Hos 2:19–20), which will come in the form of a devouring conquest of the nation by brutal foreigners, followed by exile. Yet still he seeks to win his "wife" back to faithfulness. "She . . . went after her lovers, and forgot me, says the LORD. Therefore, I will allure her . . . and speak tenderly to her" (v. 14).

Here are God's tender words to those who have rejected him: "I will espouse you for ever; I will espouse you in righteousness and justice, in steadfast love, and in mercy. I will espouse you in faithfulness, and you shall know the LORD" (Hos 2:19–20).

Jesus, the Bridegroom

Marriage is a type of covenant, and the Church Fathers saw in such passages a prophecy of God's New Covenant with his people, the Church, established through Christ. The "marriage" binding the Lord and his people is renewed through the saving sacrifice of Jesus, a covenant sealed in his blood (see Mt 26:28). Commenting on Isaiah 54:8, St. Cyril of Alexandria (c. 376–444) concludes: "'With everlasting mercy I will have compassion on you.' For the season of anger is short and brief in comparison with the measure of the boundless loving kindness given to us from God. 'He rescued us out of the power of darkness and transferred us to the kingdom of the Son of his love in light' [Col 1:13]."

"The Son of his love" is of course Jesus Christ, and the new covenant he establishes is also spoken of in terms of a "marriage" between God the Son and his people, the Church. John the Baptist is the first recorded figure in the New Testament to refer to Jesus this way. When John's disciples complain that many are leaving the Baptist to follow Jesus, John reassures them that this is how it must be.

"I am not the Christ," he reminds them, "but I have been sent before him. He who has the bride is the bridegroom; the friend of the bridegroom, who stands and hears him, rejoices greatly at the bridegroom's voice; therefore this joy of mine is now full. He must increase, but I must decrease" (Jn 3:25–30).

In great humility, John is speaking of Jesus as the groom, and himself, we might say, as only the best man at the wedding. For the moment, John seems to be using wedding imagery simply to explain that Jesus is the central character in what God is presently doing, not himself. But before long, we hear similar language describing Jesus in a much broader context (Mk 2:18–20).

JESUS CALLS HIMSELF THE BRIDEGROOM

One day some people come to Christ and ask him why the Pharisees and John the Baptist's disciples practice fasting, but his own disciples do not. Echoing John's wedding language, Jesus replies: "Can the wedding guests fast while the bridegroom is with them? As long as they have the bridegroom with them, they cannot fast. The days will come, when the bridegroom is taken away from them, and then they will fast in that day" (Mk 2:19–20).

Our Lord is explaining that his disciples will practice fasting to do penance and strengthen their prayers after he has ascended into heaven. But just as importantly, by calling himself the "bridegroom," he presses us to ponder the meaning of this image as applied to himself.

On another occasion, Jesus is warning his disciples to be ready for his return one day as the judge who brings about "the close of the age" (the end of history). He prophesies severe catastrophes and tribulations for the world before he returns: "Therefore you must be ready; for the Son of man is coming at an hour you do not expect" (Mt 24:44).

To emphasize his point, Christ follows up with parables that illustrate the importance of readiness. In one of these, he portrays himself again as a bridegroom (Mt 25:1–14). As we saw in chapter 1, this particular parable reflects a wedding custom of the day. In that culture, the groom would leave his betrothed wife at her home with her parents to go prepare a home for her in his native town. Once the home and the wedding feast were prepared, he would return to escort the bride back there for the feast.

The maids in the parable light their lamps to go out to greet the groom and accompany him to the marriage feast. But the groom is delayed, and some of the maids run out of oil. When they return home for more, they miss the groom's arrival and cannot take part in the feast.

THE MYSTERY OF CHRIST AND HIS CHURCH

The warning is clear: Be ready when Jesus returns. But why do John and Jesus speak of our Lord as a bridegroom? What meaning lies in that imagery beyond the immediate points they are making about John's status, Jesus's ascension, and Jesus's return in glory?

The Apostle Paul delves more deeply into this mystery when he provides Christian husbands and wives with instruction about how to love each other. He draws several parallels between husbands and Christ, and between wives and the Church, in how they should behave toward each other (Eph 5:25–33). In drawing these parallels, he paints a beautiful portrait of Christ's love for the Church.

To the Church, Christ is a husband who has loved her to the point of giving his life for her so that he could sanctify her (make her holy). He has cleansed her with water and the word (a reference to Baptism) to make her beautiful, full of "splendor," so that she can become his bride "without spot or wrinkle or . . . blemish" (Eph 5:27). He "nourishes and cherishes her" (v. 29).

All in all, the Apostle says, this relationship of Christ and his Church as husband and wife "is a great mystery" (Eph 5:32), no doubt worthy of deep reflection. But at the very least, we can learn from this passage that to understand something of Christ's love for us, we should think of a husband's love at its most perfect—selfless, life-giving, undying.

THE WEDDING SUPPER OF THE LAMB

The mystery is further unveiled in the book of Revelation, where we encounter in John's glorious vision a heavenly celebration unlike any other. John hears what sounds like "the voice of a great multitude, like the sound of many waters [think the roar of the ocean or a majestic waterfall], like the sound of mighty thunderpeals" (Rv 19:6). What spectacular event are they announcing? They cry out: "'Hallelujah! For the Lord our God the Almighty reigns. Let us rejoice and exult and give him the glory, for the marriage of the Lamb has come, and his bride has made herself ready; it was granted to her to be clothed with fine linen, bright and pure'—for the fine linen is the righteous deeds of the saints" (Rv 19:6–8).

The Lamb, of course, is Jesus Christ, and his Bride is the Church.

The Old Testament prophetic summons was to an adulterous wife in a long-established marriage, calling her to repent and return to her divine Husband. Here we see instead, as in Jesus's parable, a new marriage covenant. The terms "bride" and "Bridegroom" emphasize that the marriage is just beginning, finding its consummation in "the marriage [wedding] supper of the Lamb" (Rv 19:9).

Note that Paul's words to the Ephesians emphasize the work of *Christ* in preparation for this marriage: By grace, he cleanses her, beautifies her, and nourishes her through the sacraments so that he might present her to himself in the splendor of holiness. But John's vision emphasizes the role of the *Church* in preparation for this marriage, which is also essential: She "has made herself ready" by dressing herself in the white wedding gown of "righteous deeds" (Rv 19:7–8).

The angel says to John, "Write this: Blessed are those who are invited to the marriage supper of the Lamb'" (Rv 19:7). Who receives the invitation to this supper? The Christian faithful. We are called both to the blessed table of the Eucharist, which is our foretaste of glory even now, and also to the final, eternal consummation of our union with Christ in heaven, when we will at last see him "as he is," "face to face" (1 Jn 3:2; 1 Cor 13:12).

In all these New Testament passages, we find a beautiful, hope-filled vision of the union of Christ and his Church, Bridegroom and Bride, Husband and Wife. And even in the Old Testament passages foreshadowing the new marriage covenant of the Lamb with his saints, God's mercy toward his adulterous wife gives hope to those who belong to the New Covenant but have failed to live according to its life-giving provisions.

BRIDEGROOM OF THE SOUL

The scriptural figure of the divine Husband implies one additional aspect: Christ as the Bridegroom, not just of the Church as a whole, but of the individual soul as well. Though such a title is not explicit in Scripture, some biblical passages seem to hint at a kind of spiritual intimacy between the soul and Christ that could be spoken of as nuptial.

Jesus's words to his disciples on the night he was betrayed suggest a deep intimacy: "I will come again and will take you to myself, that where I am, you may be also" (Jn 14:3).

The Apostle Paul writes to the Corinthians about the individual believer's spiritual union with Christ in a way that seems to suggest a parallel (though not, of course, an equivalence) with sexual union. "Do you not know," he asks, "that he who joins himself to a prostitute becomes one body with her? For as it is written, 'The two shall become one' [Gn 2:24]. But he who is united to the Lord becomes one spirit with him" (1 Cor 6:16–17). St. Bernard of Clairvaux (1090–1153), among others, notes this parallel (*Commentary on the Song of Songs,* 31.6).

The notion that the individual soul can be wed to Christ is

well known in the lives of the saints. Teresa of Ávila, Catherine of Siena, Catherine of Alexandria, Rose of Lima, and others were all reported to have experienced a "mystical marriage" with Christ. Both Teresa and John of the Cross write of a "mystical marriage," referring to a mystical union with God that provides the most exalted condition a soul can possibly attain in this life.

THE BRIDEGROOM IN THE SONG OF SONGS

St. Bernard writes extensively and lyrically about the individual soul as the bride of Christ. In the Old Testament, the book of love poetry called the Song of Songs (or the Song of Solomon) celebrates the nuptial love of a royal Bridegroom and his bride. The work has long been viewed by Christian interpreters as an allegory of Christ's love for the Church. But Bernard (along with others, such as St. John of the Cross) sees in it as well a mystical description of the love between Christ and the soul who is ravished by his beauty.

"We must conclude, then," he observes, "that it was a special divine impulse that inspired these songs of Solomon that now celebrate the praises of Christ and his Church, the gift of holy love, the sacrament of endless union with God. Here too are expressed the mounting desires of the soul, an exultation of spirit poured forth in figurative language pregnant with delight" (*Commentary on the Song of Songs,* 1.8).

Bernard notes, for example, the monk whose devotions "make him ripe for marriage" to Christ, a soul who is "truly prepared for nuptial union with the divine Partner" (*Commentary on the Song of Songs,* 1.12). Yet "Christ will not reveal himself in this way to every person, even momentarily, but only to the one who is proved to be a worthy bride by intense devotion, vehement desire, and the sweetest affection. And the Word who comes to visit will be clothed in beauty, in every aspect a Bridegroom" (32.3).

Bernard's reference to the beauty of the Bridegroom recalls the words of the Bride in the Song of Songs, who delights in his beauty. The handsome face of the royal Bridegroom is "radiant and ruddy, distinguished among ten thousand." His appearance is like ivory and alabaster, fine gold and precious jewels. He stands tall and powerful like the great, choice cedars of Lebanon. The bride breathlessly concludes, "He is altogether desirable! This is my beloved, and this is my friend" (Sg 5:10–16).

In the book of Revelation, we find a similar kind of praise for Christ, the Bridegroom of the marriage feast. In John's vision, he is celebrated as brilliant and mighty (Rv 19:11–16).

THE BEAUTY OF CHRIST ON THE CROSS

Yes, the face of Christ the Bridegroom is beautiful in his holiness. And nowhere do we see the glory of our Lord's goodness more magnificently displayed than on the Cross.

On the Cross? But surely, someone might object, his beauty is in that place most fully obscured. Didn't Isaiah the prophet say of Christ, the Suffering Servant, "He had no beauty that we should desire him" (Is 53:2)?

Certainly a bruised, swollen, blood-covered face appears repugnant according to the world's standard of beauty. But we don't behold this face with the eyes of the world. We see through the eyes of faith, seeking the beauty of holiness, the radiance of goodness, the majesty of love. And it is on the Cross that we behold most clearly the shining glory of the Lamb of God, who takes away the sins of the world.

This is why St. Paul speaks of the Bridegroom as the One "who loved the Church and gave himself up for her" (Eph 5:25). This is why, when the book of Revelation portrays Jesus the Bridegroom at the marriage supper with his Bride, he is "the Lamb who had been slain," the same Lamb "clothed in a robe dipped in blood" (Rv 5:12; 19:13).

The Church Fathers saw the birth of the Church fore-shadowed in the blood and water that flowed from Christ's body on the cross when the Roman soldier pierced his side (Jn 19:34). The water and blood that gushed forth, they believed, represent the sacraments of love that give life to the Church: Baptism and the Eucharist. Without them she has no earthly existence.

Precisely in this bloody scene, the Fathers thus saw nuptial imagery. They noted that St. Paul once spoke of Jesus as the "second" or "last" Adam (1 Cor 15:45–47). Just as the first Adam's wife, Eve, had been taken from his side in Eden (see Gn 2:21–22), so the second Adam's wife, the Church, issued forth from his side on the Cross.

That precious blood is the emblem of his love for his Bride the Church, his love for each one of us. And so the face of the crucified Christ is in fact the face of the Bridegroom at its most beautiful.

SCRIPTURAL PASSAGES TO PONDER

John 3:25–30; Ephesians 5:25–33; Isaiah 54:5–8; Hosea 2:19–20; Mark 2:18–20; Matthew 25:1–13; Revelation 19:5–9; 21:1–5; Song of Songs 2:1–4, 10–13; 5:10, 16

O Lord, I am not worthy
That thou shouldst come to me,
But speak the words of comfort,
My spirit healed shall be,
And humbly I'll receive thee,
The Bridegroom of my soul;
No more by sin to grieve thee,
Or fly thy sweet control.

FROM "O LORD, I AM NOT WORTHY"

13

BREAD OF LIFE

*I am the bread of life; he who
comes to me shall not hunger.*

JOHN 6:35

Bread. What kind of nourishment is more basic, more universal, more traditional than bread? It's among the most ancient of human foods. Archaeologists have discovered loaves in the tombs of Egyptian Pharaohs, and wheat for making bread in the remains of settlements from eight thousand years ago. Today it remains popular worldwide, whether made from wheat, corn, barley, or some other kind of grain.

No wonder bread has been dubbed "the staff of life."

We shouldn't be surprised, then, to find that bread figures prominently throughout Scripture. God miraculously provided nourishment for the Israelites in the desert when he sent them manna—bread that came daily from the hand of God (Ex 16:4–17).

The day came when the manna ceased, and those who ate it eventually died. But the spiritual reality that the manna foreshadowed is an eternal Food that gives eternal life. For Christ chose bread to become matter for the Eucharist, the ultimate fulfillment of the Passover.

When Jesus calls himself "the Bread of Life," then, he invites us to consider how he can nourish our souls for eternity.

MANNA, BREAD FROM HEAVEN

We have seen how the sacrifice of the Passover lamb was a foreshadowing of Christ's sacrifice to take away the sins of the world. The events surrounding ancient Israel's exodus from Egypt and journey to the Promised Land are in fact rich with foreshadowings of Gospel realities.

Moses foreshadows Christ, as does the bronze serpent Moses set up in the wilderness at God's command (Nm 21:4–9; Jn 3:14). The burning bush Moses encountered on the mountain (Ex 3:1—4:17) foreshadows Mary, as does the Ark of the Covenant carried by the people through the wilderness (Ex 25:10–22). The crossing of the Red Sea (Ex 14; 1 Cor 10:1–2) foreshadows Baptism.

As slaves in Egypt, the ancient Hebrews are certainly familiar with wheat bread—a basic food consumed both by poor slaves and opulent kings in that land. But once Pharaoh, the ruler, has finally freed them to return to the Promised Land, they soon encounter on their journey another kind of bread that they don't recognize. In fact, its substance comes not from the fields, but from the wilderness, provided by the hand of God himself, and it, too, will be a foreshadowing of things to come.

Not long after the Israelites make their Exodus from

Egypt and cross the Red Sea, the people lack water suitable to drink. They complain, and the Lord provides the water they need (Ex 15:22–25). Soon after, they run out of food, and again they complain. So the Lord promises them: "Behold, I will rain bread from heaven for you" (Ex 16:4).

How does God fulfill this promise? The book of Exodus tells us that the next morning, and each morning following, there appears with the dew across the landscape "a fine, flake-like thing, fine as hoarfrost on the ground. . . . It [is] like coriander seed, white, and the taste of it [is] like wafers made with honey" (Ex 16:14, 31). The people gather it daily, grind it in mills or crush it in mortars to make a kind of flour, then boil it to make cakes. Prepared this way, it tastes like "cakes baked with oil" (Nm 11:6–9).

When the people see this substance, they have no idea what it is. They ask one another, "What is it?" which in Hebrew sounds like "man hu"—that is, *manna,* as the Greek translation renders it. So Moses tells them, "It is the bread which the LORD has given you to eat" (Ex 16:15).

Several speculations have attempted to attribute this phenomenon to natural causes. However God brings it about, he miraculously causes the manna to appear daily (except for Sabbath days) for forty years as they journey through the wilderness. It ceases to appear only when the Israelites arrive in a place where the land provides natural food, at the border of the land God has promised to give them (Ex 16:35).

AN ABIDING SYMBOL OF GOD'S CARE

After the manna ceases, in the memory of the nation it becomes a symbol of God's miraculous power, faithfulness, and providential care. It reminds his people that he graciously nourishes and sustains them day by day, that they are fed abundantly by his gracious hand, and that they are utterly dependent on him.

Later references to manna in the Old Testament elaborate on its meaning in this way. The book of Wisdom calls it the "food of angels," addressing God: "Without their toil you supplied them from heaven with bread ready to eat, providing every pleasure and suited to every taste. For your sustenance manifested your sweetness toward your children" (Ws 16:20–21). The "sweetness" of the honey-flavored wafers reveals the "sweetness" of God toward his children.

When the psalmist recalls God's mighty acts of goodness to Israel, rebuking the people for their ingratitude, he includes the miracle of the manna: "He commanded the skies above, and opened the doors of heaven; and he rained down upon them manna to eat, and gave them the grain of heaven. Man ate of the bread of angels; he sent them food in abundance" (Ps 78:23–25).

THE MANNA FORESHADOWS JESUS

In the New Testament, this "grain of heaven," this "bread of the angels," provides the historical and spiritual background for the sixth chapter of John's Gospel. In the first part of that chapter, a multitude of hungry people are once again fed bread miraculously by the hand of God, though this time the food he provides is multiplied barley loaves rather than manna (Jn 6:1–15). After a brief episode in which Jesus walks on water, demonstrating again his divine power over nature (vv. 16–21), our Lord preaches what has come to be known as the "Bread of Life Discourse," referring explicitly to the Old Testament manna in speaking of his identity and mission (vv. 22–71).

John notes that when the events he is reporting take place, the feast of the Passover is at hand (Jn 16:4). Throughout his Gospel, John's references to Jewish festivals always have a significance for the deeper meaning of the story he tells. As we saw in chapter 3, the sacrifice of the Passover lamb is a foreshadowing of Christ's sacrifice on the Cross. John is hinting that the next events in his account will point to our Lord's sacrifice and, as we shall see, the Eucharist that his sacrifice makes possible.

One day the multitudes who surround Jesus to hear his teaching and witness his miracles follow him to a remote place. No source of food available is sufficient to supply the thousands who have gathered (Jn 6:1–7). Or so it seems.

A young lad generously offers the food he has with him— five loaves of bread and two fish—and Jesus takes them. He gives thanks to his Father (blessing the meager provisions) and distributes them to the hungry people, about five thousand of them. The food miraculously multiplies, and the people eat their fill. At Jesus's command, the disciples gather up the leftovers, and the fragments of the loaves fill twelve baskets (Jn 6:1–13). Perhaps each of the twelve Apostles has filled a basket.

Manna Foreshadows the Eucharist

John's report of this miracle echoes the language that the other three Gospels and also St. Paul use to describe the institution of the Eucharist: Jesus takes, blesses (or gives thanks as part of a blessing), breaks, and gives the bread (Mt 26:26; Mk 14:22; Lk 22:19; 1 Cor 11:25). Again, John is hinting at the Eucharistic meaning of what is taking place: It is a foreshadowing of the Eucharist, which Jesus will be speaking about soon.

The people are astounded by the miracle, and they say, "This is the prophet who is to come into the world!" (Jn 6:14). Moses once spoke to the Israelites about a prophet to come in later times: "The Lord your God will raise up for you a prophet like me from among you, from your brethren—him shall you heed" (Dt 18:15). Among the Jews, various interpretations were given to Moses's words: Some thought it referred to his successor, Joshua; some, to the prophet Samuel; others to the later movement of prophets as a whole.

In Jesus's time, some seem to think that the prophet like Moses is still to come and is either the Messiah or someone like him (Jn 1:21). Jesus's followers come to agree that the prophecy does indeed refer to Jesus Christ, the Messiah. After Christ's ascension into heaven, the Apostle Peter preaches on the day of Pentecost that Jesus is in fact the prophet that Moses said would come (Acts 3:22–23). St. Stephen implies the same when he preaches in Jerusalem on the day of his martyrdom (7:37). Christ is actually prophet, priest, and king—the threefold office, as it is called, that describes his mission.

After performing the miracle, Jesus crosses to the other side of the Sea of Galilee, a journey that involves his miraculous walking on water (Jn 6:16–21). The next day, the crowds follow him. Jesus addresses them first with a warning.

They are seeking him, he observes, not because they recognized the miracle as a sign pointing to his identity, but because he provided for them to eat their fill (Jn 6:26). "Do not labor for the food that perishes," Jesus warns them, "but for the food which endures to eternal life, which the Son of man will give to you" (v. 27).

BREAD OF HEAVEN

In our Lord's preaching that follows, he first challenges his listeners to believe in him. They demand a miraculous sign (as if the earlier multiplication of food is not enough) in order to believe. They recall the manna, "the bread from heaven," as an example of the sign they are seeking, implicitly asking whether he can compare with Moses, who they think worked that miracle (Jn 6:30–31).

One of the themes running throughout John's Gospel, beginning with the first chapter, is the insistence that Jesus is greater than Moses. "For the Law came through Moses," John announces, "but grace and truth came through Jesus Christ" (Jn 1:17). The comparison is important—and scandalizing—for Jesus's Jewish contemporaries, for whom Moses is an incomparable servant of God: the liberator of his people, the lawgiver and teacher, the father of all the prophets.

John shows again in this passage the superiority of Jesus over Moses. Jesus responds to the listeners who ask about the manna that the miracle was not worked by Moses, but by God himself; and it is God, Jesus's Father, who can give them "the true bread from heaven. For the bread of God is that which comes down from heaven, and gives life to the world" (Jn 6: 32–33). Jesus implies that he himself is "the true bread from heaven," and not only will the Jews receive life from this bread, but the whole world as well.

In this first part of the discourse, Jesus is trying to bring his listeners to make an act of faith in him. He offers to them the truth that the manna, as great a miracle as it might have been, was only a foreshadowing of a much greater supernatural reality that they will find in him. Only when they believe in him will they be prepared to receive his difficult but necessary teaching about the Eucharist.

THE CROWDS ARE SCANDALIZED

Such life-giving bread is an offer difficult to refuse, so the people respond, "Lord, give us this bread always" (Jn 6:34). But once Jesus explains more fully what kind of "bread" he is offering, the crowds will be surprised, even scandalized, by what he says. He makes yet another startling "I AM" declaration:

> I am the bread of life; he who comes to me shall not hunger, and he who believes in me shall never thirst. ... For I have come down from heaven, not to do my own will, but the will of him who sent me; and this is the will of him who sent me, that I should lose nothing of all that he has given me, but raise it up on the last day. For this is the will of my Father, that everyone who sees the Son and believes in him should have eternal life; and I will raise him up at the last day. (Jn 6:35, 38–40)

In this compact statement, Jesus makes a series of stunning claims: He himself is the bread of life, who can keep his believers from hungering or thirsting. He has come down from heaven, sent by God. He will raise up his followers from the dead on judgment day, and give them eternal life. The roles signified by several of the names and titles we have studied are summed up in this brief declaration.

St. Augustine comments: "The Lord spoke of himself in a way that made him seem superior to Moses, for Moses never dared to say that he would give food that would never perish but would endure to eternal life. Jesus promises much more than Moses. Moses promised a kingdom, and a land flowing with milk and honey, good health and other temporal blessings . . . plenty for the belly, but food that perishes; whereas Christ promised food which never perishes but endures forever" (*Commentary on John*, 25:12).

Not surprisingly, Christ's listeners stumble over what he is saying. Even those who see him as the Messiah might find it hard to believe that he came down from heaven (implying his pre-incarnate existence), since they know him to be Mary's son and believe he is Joseph's son (Jn 6:41–42). Jesus recognizes the difficulty in accepting his claims. "No one can come to me," he observes, "unless the Father who sent me draws him" (Jn 6:44).

HIS FLESH IS FOOD

Jesus repeats his "I AM" statement: "I am the bread of life" (Jn 6:48). He repeats as well his promise of eternal life, and his claim to be the "living bread" that has come down from heaven (vv. 47, 50). Still, the most scandalous statement of all now appears: "If anyone eats of this bread, he will live for ever; and the bread which I shall give for the life of the world is my *flesh*" (v. 51, emphasis added).

The response of the crowd is predictable. Some of them ask skeptically: "How can this man give us his flesh to eat?" (Jn 6:52). If they had supposed him to be speaking figuratively, they would not be objecting. But they take him literally, and our Lord's reply makes it clear that he is indeed speaking literally.

Jesus does not back down or try to reassure them that he is only speaking in symbols. Instead, he presses the point multiple times:

> Truly, truly, I say to you, unless you eat the flesh of the Son of man and drink his blood, you have no life in you; he who eats my flesh and drinks my blood has eternal life, and I will raise him up on the last day. For my flesh is food indeed, and my blood is drink indeed. He who eats my flesh and drinks my blood abides in me and I in him. As the living Father sent me, and I live because of the Father, so he who eats me will live because of me. (Jn 6:53–57)

After this, John tells us, many of Jesus's disciples—not just those who have gathered to listen, but those who have been following him—complain, "This is a hard saying; who can listen to it?" (Jn 6:60). Some of them actually walk away and no longer follow him (v. 66).

If Jesus were speaking only figuratively about eating his body and drinking his blood, and his disciples were misunderstanding his meaning, surely he would call them back and say, "You don't understand; I don't mean it literally. It's only a symbol." But instead, he lets them go. They have understood him clearly, and they refuse to believe him.

Meanwhile, those who remain with Jesus, willing to believe without fully understanding the how's and why's of the mystery he is describing, will eventually take part in the most gracious gift of the Eucharist. Jesus will have his followers eat his flesh and drink his blood in that marvelous Blessed

Sacrament, in which he gives them eternal life by giving them himself in the most intimate way.

"This Is My Body"

At the Passover meal that we now call the Last Supper—at the same time, the first Eucharist—our Lord gives himself this way before his betrayal and arrest. He takes bread, gives thanks (blesses it), breaks it, and gives it to his Apostles, saying solemnly: "This is my body which is given for you. Do this in remembrance of me" (Lk 22:19). Then he gives them the cup after supper: "This cup which is poured out for you is the new covenant in my blood" (v. 20).

The reality foreshadowed by the manna has come to pass: Jesus, the true bread from heaven, is giving himself for the life of the world. Those who eat his flesh and drink his blood will have eternal life. Though the appearances of bread and wine remain, the substance—the underlying reality—changes from bread and wine into Body and Blood, a change known as *transubstantiation*.

Because our Lord's human nature is not divided, his soul is united to his body, and his divine nature is inseparable from his human nature. So we who take part in this Holy Communion till the end of time receive not only his Body and Blood, but also his Soul and Divinity. Because we are receiving the Lord himself in the Eucharist, the graces received in this sacrament are many.

We receive in the Blessed Sacrament an unparalleled intimacy with Jesus: We abide in him, and he abides in us (Jn 6:56). The graces received in Baptism are preserved, increased, and renewed, because we are sharing in the divine life of the

Second Person of the Blessed Trinity. We are also more intimately united to others in the Church: "Because there is one bread, we who are many are one body, for we all partake of the one bread" (1 Cor 10:17). And we are nourished and empowered, as members of his body, to go out and serve the world.

Two thousand years later, our Lord's table is still set for us, every day, at the Holy Sacrifice of the Mass. Just as physical food is necessary to sustain the life of the body, the spiritual food of the Eucharist is essential to nourish the life of our souls. "He who eats this bread will live for ever" (Jn 6:58). Are we hungry to receive Jesus, the Bread of Life?

SCRIPTURAL PASSAGES TO PONDER

Exodus 16:4, 9–17; Wisdom 16:20–21; Psalms 78:23–25; John 6:1–14; 30–59

O come, all you who labor
In sorrow and in pain,
Come eat this Bread from heaven;
Thy peace and strength regain.
O Jesus, we adore thee,
Our Victim and our Priest,
Whose precious Blood and Body
Become our sacred Feast!

FROM "O SACRAMENT, MOST HOLY"

14

GOOD SHEPHERD

I am the good shepherd; I know my
own and my own know me.

JOHN 10:14

The catacombs of Rome are like underground cities carved
in stone and filled with tombs. Many followers of Christ were
buried there in the early centuries of the Church, and the
tombs were often decorated with Christian imagery.

In these catacombs, the most popular artistic depiction of
Christ himself is the Good Shepherd. The images illustrate a
title that Jesus chose for himself, as recorded in John's Gospel
(Jn 10:14). He compared his loving concern for his people to
the care of a faithful shepherd for his sheep.

No wonder those who were bereaved found the theme
so comforting: In faith, they committed their departed loved
ones to the Good Shepherd, who would lead them, as the
psalmist once said, to "dwell in the house of the LORD for
ever" (Ps 23:6).

Shepherding is one of the world's oldest occupations,

dating back at least five thousand years. In biblical times, the shepherd was a well-known figure, whose demanding and sometimes dangerous labors provided milk, cheese, meat, wool, and animals for sacrifice. Several prominent scriptural characters at one time or another cared for flocks: Abraham, Jacob, Rachel, Joseph's brothers, Moses, David, and Amos.

In addition, biblical writers sometimes referred to both civil and spiritual leaders as shepherds. The Lord himself is portrayed more than once as a Shepherd who cares for his people. When Jesus calls himself "the good shepherd," then, and God's people, his sheep, his listeners can draw on a rich spiritual and cultural tradition to ponder his meaning.

THE SHEPHERD AS NURTURER

The familiar figure of the shepherd thus appears throughout Scripture, especially in the Old Testament. Some form of the word "shepherd" appears more than a hundred times in the Bible. Not only the familiarity of the role, but also its distinctive characteristics, make it suitable for symbolizing the relationship of civil and religious leaders to their subjects, and of God to his people.

In the biblical context, the shepherd's first responsibility is to nourish his sheep by providing adequate food and water. They are not fed in pens; they must forage for their food and drink. So they must travel from pasture to pasture, water source to water source.

Goats are capable of seeking out the best feeding grounds, but sheep are known for their helplessness in the search for nourishment. They must be led by shepherds to green pastures and water supplies. More than most other domesticated species, they also need help in finding their way back home, because they are easily lost.

THE SHEPHERD AS PROTECTOR

The shepherd's second responsibility, then, is to protect his sheep. He must keep them from straying, getting separated from the rest of the flock, and wandering into dangerous places where they might fall or become trapped. He provides special, tender attention to the young and feeble of the flock.

The shepherd's staff, with its crook (one end shaped like a hook), extends the shepherd's reach. So he uses it to steer the sheep and even rescue them from places difficult to reach with his arm.

Because sheep are defenseless, the shepherd must defend them against predators such as lions, bears, and wolves, as well as protect them from venomous snakes. Because sheep are valuable, the shepherd must also guard them from thieves. The shepherd's rod, a thick wooden stick, can be used as a bludgeon to protect the sheep against all these enemies.

THE SHEPHERD AS GUIDE,
GUARD, AND HEALER

The shepherd's typical day begins early in the morning with leading the flock out to pasture, walking ahead of the sheep instead of driving them from behind. When they reach the intended location, they feed on the grass all day as the shepherd keeps careful watch. Occasionally a sheep strays, and the shepherd must go out, search for it diligently, and bring it back to the flock.

The shepherd must also lead the sheep to drink, either from natural streams or springs or from troughs connected to man-made wells. If a well has no trough, he must dip his cup in it and give each sheep a drink from it.

In the evening, the shepherd must lead his flock back home to the sheepfold. He causes the sheep to pass under his rod, one at a time, into the entrance of the fold. That way he can count them and make sure all are accounted for.

The shepherd's responsibilities continue through the night. He must guard them from predators and thieves in the darkness. He may sleep with his body across the entrance to the fold, with his rod and staff close at hand as weapons to defend them from their enemies.

Sheep fall prey to biting flies, lice, and ticks, which torment them especially on their heads, burrowing into their ears and noses. These vermin are not simply irritating; their bites can cause illness and even death. So the shepherd makes a mixture containing olive oil and anoints their heads with it, rubbing it into their wool and on their face. In ancient times, oil is also poured on a wound to promote healing.

RULERS AS SHEPHERDS

Keeping in mind these characteristics of the shepherd and his role, we can see why spiritual and civil leaders in Scripture are often compared to shepherds, and their subjects to sheep. Rulers must lead the people, provide for their welfare (whether bodily or spiritual), and defend them.

God speaks of Joshua, who leads the Israelites in their conquest of Canaan, the Promised Land, as the one who shepherds them (Nm 27:18). He refers in the same way to

the judges who rule the people before the kingdom is established (2 Sm 7:7; 1 Chr 17:6); King David (2 Sm 5:2; 1 Chr
11:2; Ps 78:71); and the civil and spiritual rulers (kings and
priests) of the later kingdoms (Jer 22:22; Ez 34:10). Through
the prophet Isaiah, the Lord even refers to Cyrus, the pagan
Persian emperor, as his shepherd, because God uses him to
allow the people to return to their homeland from exile (Is
44:28).

Calling both rulers and deities "shepherds" was in
fact common throughout ancient Mediterranean cultures
across thousands of years. The peoples of Mesopotamia, the
Egyptians (whose written sign for the verb "to rule" was a
shepherd's crook), the Greeks, and the Romans all used this
familiar imagery.

THE LORD AS SHEPHERD

The Lord himself leads his people, provides for their welfare, and defends them. So he too is not surprisingly called
the Shepherd of his people. The best-known and best-loved
portrait of the Lord as a Shepherd is found in the beautiful
twenty-third Psalm (Ps 23:1–6), which Christians have trea-
sured and memorized since ancient times as a prophetic and
comforting portrait of the divine Shepherd and his providential care. It was written by King David, who himself had once
been a shepherd boy.

If we recall the details of the ancient shepherd's role that
we have reviewed—his primary responsibilities of nourishment and protection; the function of his rod and staff, oil and
cup; his personal familiarity and concern for each sheep who
belongs to him—we can meditate more deeply and fruitfully

on this psalm, and on our Lord's providential care for each of us.

This biblical title for the Lord is found in many other places as well. Israel (Abraham's grandson, also called Jacob) refers to him as "the Shepherd, the Rock of Israel" (Gn 49:24). The psalmists call to him: "Give ear, O Shepherd of Israel, you who lead Joseph like a flock" (Ps 80:1). "O save your people, and bless your heritage; be their shepherd and carry them for ever" (Ps 28:9).

The prophet Micah cries out to the Lord: "Shepherd your people with your staff, the flock of your inheritance" (Mi 7:14). And God himself promises through the prophet Jeremiah: "I will lead them back, I will make them walk by brooks of water, in a straight path in which they shall not stumble . . . [I] will gather [Israel], and will keep him as a shepherd keeps his flock" (Jer 31:9–10).

EVIL SHEPHERDS

When the people lack leadership, they are often described in the Old Testament as sheep without a shepherd (2 Chr 18:6; Zec 10:2). God laments such a situation through the prophet Ezekiel: "So they were scattered, because there was no shepherd; and they became food for all the wild beasts. My sheep were scattered; they wandered over all the mountains and on every high hill; my sheep were scattered over all the face of the earth, with none to search or seek for them" (Ez 34:5–6).

This comparison is echoed in the Gospels: "When [Jesus] saw the crowds, he had compassion for them, because they were harassed and helpless, like sheep without a shepherd" (Mt 9:36; also Mk 6:34).

When the shepherds are negligent, the flock suffers. God reprimands the careless shepherds: "The weak you have not strengthened, the sick you have not healed, the crippled you have not bound up, the strayed you have not brought back, the lost you have not sought" (Ez 34:4).

Sometimes the shepherds of the people are worse than simply absent or negligent. First, they actively mislead the people into barren or dangerous places:"My people have been lost sheep," the Lord declares;"their shepherds have led them astray, turning them away on the mountains; from mountain to hill they have gone; they have forgotten their fold" (Jer 50:6). The kings and even some of the priests of this time led the people into idolatry, the worshipping of false gods.

Second, rather than feeding the sheep, the shepherds exploit the flock to feed themselves. God rebukes them:"The shepherds also have no understanding; they have all turned to their own way, each to his own gain, one and all" (Is 56:11–12). "Ho, shepherds of Israel who have been feeding yourselves! Should not shepherds feed the sheep? You eat the fat; you clothe yourselves with the wool . . . but you do not feed the sheep" (Ez 34:2–3). The leaders are busy amassing wealth for themselves instead of serving the people.

Third, rather than leading the sheep gently, the shepherds rule over them as tyrants: "With force and harshness," God tells them, "you have ruled" the sheep (Ez 34:4).

Worst of all, rather than protecting the people, the shepherds themselves become the predators of the flock. "You slaughter the fatlings," the Lord declares to them (Ez 34:3). "I will rescue my sheep from [your] mouths, that they may not be food for [you]" (v. 10). The ravenous rulers appropriate for themselves the goods of others.

In this extended lament and rebuke, delivered through the prophet Ezekiel (born c. 623 BC), God has thus cataloged the failings of the civil and spiritual leaders of Israel in the period before their defeat and exile by the Neo-Babylonian empire. Then he prophesies their judgment and punishment: "Behold, I am against the shepherds!" (Ez 34:10).

THE PROMISED SHEPHERD

Nevertheless, the Lord also offers hope to the people they have abused: The day is coming when he himself will do for them as a Shepherd what their shepherds have failed to do.

"For thus says the LORD God: Behold, I, I myself, will search for my sheep, and will seek them out. . . . I will rescue them . . . I will feed them . . . by the fountains . . . I will make them lie down. . . . I will seek the lost, I will bring back the strayed, and I will bind up the crippled, and I will strengthen the weak, and the fat and the strong I will watch over" (Ez 34:11–16).

Not only the shepherds, but also those among the sheep who are wealthy (fat) and strong (powerful), will be scrutinized ("watched over"). The wealthy and powerful have seized the pasture for themselves, pushing out the poor and the weak. So God declares: "Behold, I, I myself, will judge between the fat sheep and the lean sheep" (Ez 34:20).

How will the Lord care for his people this way? "I will set over them one Shepherd, my servant David, and he shall feed them; he shall feed them and be their shepherd. And I, the LORD, will be their God, and my servant David shall be prince among them; I, the LORD, have spoken" (Ez 34:23–24).

Calling the shepherd-prince to come "David" is of course

a Messianic reference. (Recall the study of Messianic titles in chapter 2.) It occurs in other biblical passages as well (Jer 30:9; Hos 3:5). When the Messiah comes, he will replace the false shepherds and serve God's people as their true shepherd. Note that the two promises God makes here—that the Lord himself will be their shepherd, and that the Messiah to come will be their one shepherd—taken together imply that the Messiah will be God himself.

The prophet Isaiah makes a similar promise: "Behold, the LORD comes," the prophet announces. "He will feed his flock like a shepherd, he will gather the lambs in his arms, he will carry them in his bosom, and gently lead those that are with young" (Is 40:10–11).

The image here is especially tender. When a pregnant ewe leaves the flock to give birth, the shepherd must accompany her to guard her during her vulnerable moments of delivery. After the lamb is born, he carries it back to the flock. For several days, until the lamb learns to walk, the shepherd may carry it in his arms or in the loose folds of his cloak.

Jesus As the Promised Shepherd

This passage in Isaiah is prefaced with the declaration that a voice will cry in the wilderness to "make straight in the desert a highway for our God," and that "the glory of the LORD shall be revealed, and all flesh shall see it together" (Is 40:3, 5). As Luke points out in his Gospel, this prophecy points to the ministry of John the Baptist in preparing the people for Christ (Lk 3:1–6)—with the implication that the gentle shepherd to come is Christ.

The Gospels of Matthew (26:31) and Mark (14:27) report

that Jesus cites yet another Old Testament prophecy of a shepherd, found in the book of Zechariah, as a reference to himself
and his coming passion: "Strike the shepherd, that the sheep
may be scattered" (Zec 13:7).

All these biblical references provide a rich background,
then, to Jesus's statement: "I am the good shepherd" (Jn
10:14). The kings and priests of the Old Covenant have failed
miserably in their role as shepherds. God has promised that he
himself will become their shepherd to care for them, that the
Messiah will be their shepherd-prince. Now the Shepherd, the
Messianic Shepherd, the divine Shepherd, has finally come.

GUARDING THE WAY

In the passage following, Jesus offers his disciples what has
come to be known as "the Discourse of the Good Shepherd"
(Jn 10:1–18). The Lord speaks first of someone who, instead
of trying to "enter the sheepfold by the door," tries to climb
in "by another way." Such an intruder is "a thief and a rob-
ber" (v. 1).

"I am the door," Jesus goes on to say; "if any one enters by
me, he will be saved, and will go in and out to find pasture.
The thief comes only to steal and kill and destroy; I came that
they may have life, and have it abundantly" (Jn 10:9–10).

We have seen how the ancient shepherd sometimes slept
with his body across the entrance to the sheepfold to protect
the sheep from nighttime intruders. In a sense, then, he serves
as the security "door" to the fold.

But he also serves as the "door" in the sense of the
"doorway" or entryway. In commenting on this passage,
St. John Chrysostom teaches that Christ is the "door" into

the sheepfold in that he "introduces us to the Father." The "thieves and robbers" are the antichrist, the false christs, and the heretics who claim to show some other way to salvation (*Homilies on the Gospel of John*, 59.2–3).

THE GOOD SHEPHERD

Now Jesus makes the statement that identifies him as the fulfillment of Ezekiel's prophecies and of Zechariah's as well: "I am the good shepherd. The good shepherd lays down his life for the sheep" (Jn 10:11). His passion and death are approaching; once again he is seeking to prepare his disciples for the horror to come.

Jesus emphasizes repeatedly, as John's Gospel records (Jn 14:30–31; 19:11, 30), that he is not the powerless prey of his enemies, nor the hapless victim of circumstances beyond his control. He willingly lays his life down in order to fulfill God's plan of salvation, which requires that the shepherd be struck down.

"For this reason the Father loves me, because I lay down my life, that I may take it again [that is, rise from the dead]. No one takes it from me, but I lay it down of my own accord. I have power to lay it down, and I have power to take it again; this charge I have received from my Father" (Jn 10:17–18).

Next Jesus speaks of the "hireling"—the mercenary shepherd who has no personal investment in the sheep. The hireling does not love the sheep; they do not belong to him. So he is unwilling to sacrifice himself to protect them; he cares only about his wages.

"He who is a hireling and not a shepherd, whose own the sheep are not, sees the wolf coming and leaves the sheep and flees, and the wolf snatches them and scatters them. He flees because he is a hireling and cares nothing for the sheep" (Jn 10:12–13). We can imagine that he is describing some of the faithless civil and spiritual leaders of his time.

"I Know My Own"

Jesus then repeats his solemn statement, "I am the good shepherd," and offers another characteristic of his relationship to the sheep that distinguishes him from the hirelings: "I know my own and my own know me, as the Father knows me and I know the Father" (Jn 10:14–15). In ancient times, the shepherds know their sheep well; they can distinguish between them in appearance and temperament, and they often give them personal names. To the good shepherd, his sheep are not mere numbers; they are individuals.

For their part, because of this close relationship with the shepherd, the sheep recognize his voice and respond to his call. This natural bond of trust is reflected in Jesus's first comments about the sheep in this discourse: "The sheep hear [the shepherd's] voice, and he calls his own sheep by name and leads them out. When he has brought out all his own, he goes before them, and the sheep follow him, for they know his voice. A stranger they will not follow, but will flee from him, for they do not know the voice of strangers" (Jn 10:3–5).

Shepherd and Guardian of Souls

Shortly afterward, Jesus says to his adversaries, no doubt with sadness, "You do not believe, because you do not belong to my sheep" (Jn 10:26).

To those who are his own, however, the Lord makes a comforting promise: "I give them eternal life, and they shall never perish; and no one shall snatch them out of my hand" (Jn 10:29). Like the strong and diligent shepherd who protects his sheep from the wolves, lions, and bears, Jesus defends his followers from their spiritual enemies.

However close the Devil might creep to the flock, if the sheep stay close at hand, right beside their Shepherd, that ancient predator cannot snatch them from their Protector's firm hold. Nevertheless, if they willingly stray from the shepherd, they may make themselves vulnerable.

Jesus's consoling words about being our shepherd are echoed elsewhere in the New Testament. The writer of Hebrews calls him "that great shepherd of the sheep" (Heb 13:20). Peter comforts us, those who are the Lord's flock, with a reminder of our past and a promise for our future: "You were straying like sheep, but have now returned to the Shepherd and Guardian of your souls. . . . And when the Chief Shepherd is manifested you will obtain the unfading crown of glory" (1 Pt 2:25; 5:1–4).

Scriptural Passages to Ponder

Psalms 23:1–6; 80:1–3; Ezekiel 34:11–16; 25–31; Isaiah 40:9–11; John 10:1–18, 27–29; Hebrews 13:20–21; 1 Peter 2:21–25; 5:1–4

The King of love my shepherd is,
Whose goodness faileth never;
I nothing lack if I am his,
And he is mine forever.
Where streams of living water flow

My ransomed soul he leadeth,
And where the verdant pastures grow
With food celestial feedeth.
And so through all the length of days
Thy goodness faileth never,
Good Shepherd, may I sing thy praise
Within thy house forever.

FROM HENRY W. BAKER, "THE KING
OF LOVE MY SHEPHERD IS"

Portraits of Jesus:
His Life in Us

TRUE VINE

*I am the true vine, and my
Father is the vinedresser.*

JOHN 15:1

"The vineyard of the LORD of hosts is the house of Israel" (Is 51:7). The people of God in the Old Testament are sometimes compared to a choice grapevine or vineyard that has been planted and cultivated by the Lord. But because of their sins, the people have failed to bear fruit. They have become instead like a wild and barren vine. In chastisement, God allows the unruly plant to be uprooted and trampled upon by the nation's enemies.

The prophets poignantly lament this judgment, and the psalmist cries out to God, asking him to restore the vine. In his mercy, the Lord finally answers that prayer by establishing a new vine: His Son, Jesus Christ, becomes "the true vine" (Jn 15:1). He is the source of life for all who are intimately joined to him as branches of that luxurious vine.

THE OLD TESTAMENT VINEYARD

When the Israelites cross the wilderness under Moses and arrive at Canaan, the Promised Land, God commands Moses to send men to spy out the land. When the spies return, as evidence of the land's fertility they bring back with them the branch of a grapevine. It has a cluster of grapes so large that two men must carry it on a pole between them (Nm 13:21–24).

Centuries later, in the brief period of Jewish independence from foreign powers during the second century BC, the Maccabean rulers mint coins with vines to symbolize the Jewish nation. Many synagogues in ancient times bear carvings of grapes on their front exterior. Even today, a depiction of two men carrying a cluster of grapes on a pole is a symbol of the modern nation of Israel.

The soil of this land is favorable to the cultivation of grapes. In biblical times, in the higher elevations, vineyards are planted in stone-walled terraces (Jer 31:5). But cultivated grapes also flourish in the lowland plains. The grapevine comes to represent prosperity for the Jewish people, and vintage time—when the grapes are harvested and the juice is pressed out to make wine—becomes a joyous season, with singing and dancing.

A closer look at the cultivation and features of these ancient vineyards provides a useful context for understanding scriptural references to them.

CULTIVATING THE VINEYARD

The cultivation of the grapevine begins with digging a trench several feet wide around the area to be made into a vineyard

(Is 5:1–7). Thick posts are set in the trench, and to these are attached interwoven branches that will establish a hedge or fence (Mk 12:1). Thorny shrubs or trees may be planted around the vineyard for more protection from animals and thieves, and the fence may be reinforced with stones, mounds of dirt, or sun-dried bricks.

Next, the soil of the area enclosed is loosened with tools similar to hoes, and any stones in the soil are removed. Young vines to be planted are first soaked in water for several days. Then they are planted in rows about eight feet apart. Every spring, the vines are pruned with pruning hooks (Lv 25:3; Jl 3:10).

A wooden booth, called a watchtower, may be built on a high spot overlooking the vineyard in order to guard it from thieves and animals. Members of the family that owns the vineyard may take turns occupying this structure.

The grapes may be eaten fresh or dried as raisins. The juice may be drunk fresh, boiled down to make a jelly, or fermented into wine.

Winepresses, where the grapes are pressed to gather the juice for making wine, are built in or close by the vineyards. They are square or oblong and are sometimes cut in limestone, then lined with mortar or small stones.

Vintage workers fill the winepress with grapes, then tread them with their bare feet, singing and shouting as they work (Am 9:13; Is 16:10). A small hole near the bottom of one side allows the juice to flow out into a smaller basin below.

ANCIENT LAWS CONCERNING VINEYARDS

Vineyard owners sometimes rent out their vineyards to tenant farmers. According to the Law of Moses, beginning with the fifth year after planting, after each annual harvest the vineyard owner must send a servant to obtain his share of the produce (Lv 19:23–25).

Another aspect of the legal context of vineyard ownership should be kept in mind: According to ancient inheritance law of the time, if the owner of real estate has no heir, the land can be considered "ownerless property," allowing for the first claimant to take possession of it.

If a vineyard proves to be completely unproductive, efforts at cultivation cease. The vines grow wild, and weeds and briers take over the ground. Animals or marauders are allowed to occupy it. Then the dry, dead vines are gathered to use as fuel for the fire (Ez 15:1–8).

ISRAEL AS GOD'S VINEYARD

All these details of the vineyard's construction and use help us to understand more fully the Old Testament imagery of Israel as a vine. The prophet Isaiah announces, "Let me sing for my beloved a love song concerning his vineyard" (Is 5:1). The "beloved" One is the Lord, and "the vineyard of the LORD of hosts is the house [that is, the nation] of Israel" (v. 7).

Isaiah goes on to tell how God has labored faithfully to construct the vineyard. He dug the soil, cleared it of stones, planted the vines, built a watchtower, and hewed out of stone a wine vat (wine press with a basin) within it (Is 5:2).

The psalmist uses similar imagery to describe how the Lord has established the nation of Israel, noting that he brought this vine out of Egypt (in the exodus of the Hebrews led by Moses). Then he planted it in the Promised Land, after clearing the ground of rocks—that is, driving out the nations who occupied the area. The vine "took deep root and filled the land" (Ps 80:8–11).

WILD GRAPES

But there is a problem, Isaiah declares. The beloved Builder and Cultivator of the vineyard "looked for it to yield grapes, but it yielded wild grapes" rather than the useful, desirable domesticated variety he had planted (Is 5:2). The Lord "looked for justice, but behold, bloodshed; for righteousness, but behold, a cry" of complaint over the injustice of the people (v. 7).

The prophecy then shifts to the first person, with God himself speaking: "What more is there to do for my vineyard, that I have not done in it?" (Is 5:4). He calls the people of Judah and its capital city, Jerusalem—the vine he has planted—to defend their behavior, sins that have borne wild, inedible fruit rather than domesticated, delicious grapes. Of course, they cannot justify themselves.

As we have seen in prophecies studied in previous chapters, the sins of the people will lead to their chastisement, in the form of conquest, devastation, and exile by the armies of a foreign nation. The beloved vineyard Owner declares: "Now I will tell you what I will do to my vineyard. I will remove its hedge, and it shall be devoured; I will break down its wall, and it shall be trampled down. I will make it a waste; it shall not be pruned or hoed, and briars and thorns will grow up; I will also command the clouds that they rain no rain upon it" (Is 5:5–6).

Then the Lord catalogs the misdeeds of the people and predicts a fiery punishment as a consequence, at the hands of the invaders (Is 5:24–30).

The psalmist looks back on the divine punishment from the viewpoint of the exile in Babylon. He laments the devastation of the vine that God once planted, praying: "Why then have you broken down its walls, so that all who pass along the ways pluck its fruit? The boar from the forest ravages it, and all that move in the field feed on it.... They have burned it with fire, they have cut it down" (Ps 80:12–13, 16).

HOPE FOR RESTORATION

Even so, the psalmist intercedes for his people, taking hope that the Lord might restore the vineyard and cultivate once more the vine he once planted: "Turn again, O God of hosts! Look down from heaven, and see; have regard for this vine, the stock which your right hand planted.... Restore us, O LORD God of hosts! Let your face shine, that we may be saved!" (Ps 80:14–15, 19).

Note here, in the midst of the vine and vineyard imagery, words that are not clearly related to that imagery: "But let your hand [O God] be upon the man of your right hand, the son of man whom you have made strong for yourself!" (Ps 80:17).

Not surprisingly, Christian interpreters of this passage have seen here a reference to Christ, "the Son of man . . . seated at the right hand of . . . God" (Lk 22:69). Through him, the vine will be restored; the face of God will shine; and the people will be saved (Ps 80:19).

JESUS'S PARABLE OF THE WICKED TENANTS

In these Old Testament passages, we find a rich context for Jesus's parable of the wicked tenants (Mk 12:1–12). His listeners may well recall the imagery of Isaiah and the psalmist as Jesus describes a man who "planted a vineyard, and set a hedge around it, and dug a pit for the wine press, and built a tower, and let it out to tenants, and went into another country" (v. 1).

The vineyard owner, of course, is God, and the vineyard is his people. But notice that here, a new set of characters appear: the "tenant" farmers of the vineyard (Mk 12:1), those to whom God has entrusted his people. These "tenants" are the leaders of the Jewish people. The leaders do not "own" the nation; they are only workers appointed to care for it.

As we have noted, according to the Law of Moses, each year after the harvest, the vineyard owner sends a servant to receive the owner's share of the produce. Fruit is a common biblical symbol of the consequences of moral conduct, either "good fruit" or bad (Is 3:10; Jer 6:19; 17:8; Hos 10:12; Mt 7:16–20; Jn 15:2; Gal 5:22). In the parable, then, God is looking for righteous deeds from the nation.

Nevertheless, these tenants are wicked. When God sends his servants—the prophets who call the people to holiness—they refuse to give God his share of the fruit. Instead, they mistreat the prophets. Some are beaten, some are wounded and humiliated, and in this culture, humiliation can be seen as an even greater offense than physical assault. Some of the servants are even killed.

These details of the parable, of course, point to Israel's sad history of ignoring, mocking, rejecting, and abusing the prophets. Micaiah was cast into prison, where he had to survive on scant bread and water (1 Kgs 22:27). Jeremiah was beaten and placed in the stocks (Jer 20:22). Elijah's fellow prophets were put to the sword (1 Kgs 19:10); Zechariah was stoned (2 Chr 24:20–22); Isaiah, according to ancient tradition, was sawn in two (Heb 11:37).

THE OWNER SENDS HIS BELOVED SON

In the normal course of events, someone in the owner's position would almost certainly not have continued sending servants, knowing that they would all be mistreated. But the owner is God, who in his great mercy continues to give the leaders a chance to repent. In the end, then, he sends his own "beloved son" instead of a servant (Mk 12:6).

Keep in mind that throughout the Old Testament, the term "beloved son" refers to someone who is an only son, and is repeatedly applied to an only son who is destined to die (Gn 22:2; Jer 6:26; Am 8:10; Zec 12:10). Jesus is implying that he himself is that "beloved Son" of the vineyard owner, just as the Father bore witness at his baptism (Mk 1:11) and in the transfiguration (Mk 9:7). He is the heir of the Father and has come to claim the fruit of his Father's vineyard.

Given the violence against the prophets, it might seem reckless and even foolish for the Father to send his Son. But God's love is persistent in the face of rejection, and "the foolishness of God is wiser than men" (1 Cor 1:25). So he sends him in one last effort at reconciliation.

Nevertheless, the tenants see a chance to take possession of the vineyard themselves if they kill the owner's heir. So they kill him and cast his body unceremoniously out of the vineyard. They deny him even a proper burial as a final insult.

At this point, the parable becomes prophecy. Jesus is predicting his passion and death as instigated and executed by the religious and civil leaders of the people.

JESUS, THE TRUE HEIR

In this parable, then, Jesus shows himself to be the true Heir of the vineyard of God's people. Their leaders are merely tenants who have attempted to usurp him and exploit the vineyard for their own gain.

How does God respond to this final crime? "The owner [in the original Greek, literally "the lord"] of the vineyard will come and destroy the tenants, and give the vineyard to others" (Mk 12:9). In the Old Testament depictions of the vineyard of God's people, the vine itself fails to bear good fruit, so God allows it to be destroyed. But here, only the tenants—the leaders of the people—are punished, and the people are placed under the stewardship of new managers.

God's people will remain, then, in the vineyard of the Church that Jesus will establish. Their new leaders will be the Apostles, the leaders of the new Israel (Lk 22:28–30), who will care for the people of God and help them bear abundant fruit (Rom 7:4; 1 Cor 3:6–7; Col 1:3–6, 9–10).

AN INTIMATE RELATIONSHIP

Some days later, now in a private conversation, Jesus speaks once again of the vine. The lamps are burning low as the night advances. He has just celebrated the Last Supper, the first Eucharist, with his Apostles, speaking to them afterward at length in the intimate setting of the Upper Room. It is the night of his betrayal and arrest. So he reminds them of his faithful love for them, and tells them that he goes to prepare a place for them so that they can be with him forever (Jn 14:2–3).

Our Lord must now spend some time in the Garden of Gethsemane, talking with his Father to ready himself for the horrors that he knows are at hand. Jesus tells his disciples: "Rise, let us go hence" (Jn 14:31) to the familiar place where he often goes to pray. As they walk, he offers his last private discourse before he is taken away to be tortured, crucified, and buried.

The words of those who know they are about to die have a special significance. Such words typically reveal, in an unparalleled way, the heart of the one who is departing. In this moment, Jesus makes the last of his profound "I AM" statements. He once again uses the vine imagery, on the night before he dies, telling his beloved friends, "I am the true vine. . . . Abide in me, and I in you" (see Jn 15:1–17). As they walk together, our Lord goes on to elaborate on this intriguing imagery of mutual abiding.

We can't be certain of the route that Jesus and his Apostles take from the Upper Room to the Garden. Some Bible commentators believe that Jesus delivers this address on the way as they walk in the Valley of Kidron or on the side of the Mount of Olives. If so, he could very well be making use of a visual aid: an extensive vineyard covers the valley at that time.

Others believe he takes a route that night that runs by the Temple. If so, another visual aid is close at hand: The massive gates of the Temple are made of bronze, covered with gold, with great golden vines—the familiar symbol of Israel— bearing clusters of grapes as tall as a man's height.

This time, the Lord is not offering a public parable to rebuke Israel's leaders, warning them, as the prophets had done before him, of the ruin that follows spiritual and moral barrenness. Instead, he is speaking only to his close friends (Jn 15:15), focusing on the nature of the intimate relationship he desires to have with them.

"I AM THE TRUE VINE"

In this solemn address, the vine is not God's people, but rather Jesus himself: "I am the true vine, and my Father is the vinedresser" (Jn 15:1). In him, Israel is personified and finds perfection.

Yet Jesus is not replacing God's people; instead, they will become a part of the new vine through their union with him: "I am the vine," he tells them, you are the branches" (Jn 15:5). The Old Covenant is giving way to the New, and the New Covenant finds its core, its very life, in Christ himself.

In the natural world, what is the relationship of a branch to the vine from which it stems? The branch finds in the vine its origins, its vitality, and its fruitfulness. Vine and branch are a single organism.

Like a kind of lifeblood, the juice of the vine flows out to the branch to become its source of food and water and growth.

As a result, when cut off from the vine, the branch withers and dies. No longer capable of bearing fruit, it becomes fuel for fire.

"ABIDE IN ME"

In all these respects, the natural life of the vine's branches parallels the spiritual life of those joined to Christ. "Abide in me," he tells his disciples, "and I in you. As the branch cannot bear fruit by itself, unless it abides in the vine, neither can you, unless you abide in me.... He who abides in me, and I in him, he it is that bears much fruit, for apart from me you can do nothing" (Jn 15:4–5).

To abide means to remain; to stay stable or fixed in a condition; to continue in a place. In this context, we might even say that Jesus is inviting his disciples to make their permanent home in him. They must remain connected to him at the deepest level to survive spiritually, because he is the source of life for them, the channel of all God's grace, their spiritual home.

St. Cyril of Alexandria explains: "Just as the root of the vine administers and distributes to the branches the benefit of its own natural and inherent qualities, so too the only-begotten Word of God imparts to the saints, as it were, a likeness to his own nature and the nature of God the Father by giving them the Spirit, in that they have been united with him through faith and perfect holiness. Christ nourishes them in piety and works in them the knowledge of all virtue and good works" (*Commentary on John,* 10.2).

Staying Connected to Christ

How do we stay connected to Christ? "As the Father has loved me," Jesus promises, "so have I loved you; abide in my love. If you keep my commandments, you will abide in my love" (Jn 15:9–10). And what does Jesus command? "This is my commandment, that you love one another as I have loved you" (v. 12).

In his first letter, John elaborates on what it means to abide in Christ: "Whoever confesses that Jesus is the Son of God, God abides in him, and he in God. So we know and believe the love God has for us. God is love, and he who abides in love abides in God, and God abides in him" (1 Jn 4:15–16).

Through the virtues of faith and love—not just love for God, but love for others—we abide in God. St. Cyril of Alexandria reminds us that "a mere barren confession of faith" is not enough to keep us alive on the vine. We need as well "the sealing bond of our union" with Christ by "the good works that proceed from love" (*Commentary on John,* 10.2).

We are utterly dependent on Christ for the cultivation of these virtues. He has chosen and appointed us to "bear much fruit" (Jn 15:16). But if we try to bear fruit on our own, we can do nothing apart from his grace (v. 5). Worse yet, if we separate ourselves from him, we die spiritually. The Father, the vinedresser, cuts us off as a dead branch and throws us into the fire (v. 6).

Nevertheless, if we abide in Christ's grace, and in his love, we will have his own life flowing within us. If we cultivate and preserve an intimate friendship with him, a relationship of trust and obedience and reliance, he promises that his joy in us will be full. For joy, like love, is a fruit of the Holy Spirit

(Gal 5:22–23), and the Spirit is the sap, the lifeblood, that runs throughout the Vine.

SCRIPTURAL PASSAGES TO PONDER

Isaiah 5:1–7; Psalms 80:7–19; Mark 12:1–12; John 15:1–17; 1 John 2:28–29

Jesus, immutably the same,
Thou true and living Vine,
Around thy all-supporting stem
My feeble arms I twine.
Quickened by thee, and kept alive,
I flourish and bear fruit;
My life I from thy sap derive,
My vigor from thy root.

AUGUSTUS TOPLADY, "ABIDE IN ME"

16

DAWN FROM ON HIGH

The day shall dawn upon us from on high, to give light to those who sit in darkness and in the shadow of death.

LUKE 1:78–79

Few things are more essential to our physical life in this world than light.

Sunlight provides the energy that's necessary to function for most living things on our planet. Through reflected light, our eyes can perceive the reality around us, with the beauties of radiance and color. Light even has purifying properties.

Not surprisingly, then, since ancient times light has served as a symbol of certain essential spiritual realities. The Old Testament psalmists and prophets especially speak of God's gift of spiritual enlightenment—the purifying, life-giving gift that enables us to perceive reality as it truly is. In the New Testament, Jesus is declared to be the embodiment of this gift from heaven. He has dispelled our darkness; he is "the dawn . . . from on high."

PHYSICAL LIGHT

The Bible begins with light, and it ends with light.

The creation account in Genesis speaks of darkness upon the face of the deep. But immediately the Spirit of God enters to move over the darkness. The Word of God sounds forth: "Let there be light!" And light does indeed come into being, created by the Word of God (Jn 1:1–2). God sees that the light is good, and God separates the light from the darkness, calling the light "Day" (Gn 1:1–3).

Once again, the Word of God thunders forth, "Let there be lights in the firmament of the heavens to separate the day from the night, and . . . to give light upon the earth" (Gn 1:14–15). And so it happens. God creates "the greater light," the sun, "to rule the day" (v. 16). And God sees that it is good (v. 18).

The glorious creation we call light is indeed good, and "the greater light," the heavenly body we call the sun, radiates light that is essential to life on earth. Without the light of the sun, the web of life on our planet as we know it would die. And as if God wishes to remind us of the sunlight's importance, he has arranged our world so that most of us must spend at least some hours each day in the darkness of night (Gn 1:5).

The light of the sun not only makes possible our physical life; radiated and reflected, it makes possible the sense of sight. Through this light we can see the world around us, and see ourselves as well. Sunlight also bleaches and disinfects, a source of cleansing and healing.

In these ways, all the living things that God creates on earth rely on the light. Among them are the first man and woman; and the light of God fills not only the eyes of their bodies, but the eyes of their souls as well.

SPIRITUAL AND MORAL LIGHT

Given these properties of light, we can understand the frequent Old Testament imagery of illumination with regard to the moral and spiritual aspects of our world. Just as in the creation account, all physical light comes ultimately from God, the biblical authors speak of God as the source of spiritual and moral illumination as well—radiant and life-giving knowledge and wisdom: "Lift up the light of your countenance upon us, O LORD!" (Ps 4:6). "The LORD is my light and my salvation" (Ps 27:1). "For with you [O LORD] is the fountain of life; in your light do we see light" (Ps 36:9). "O send out your light and your truth; let them lead me" (Ps 43:3). "The LORD is God, and he has given us light" (Ps 118:27). "O house of Jacob, come, let us walk in the light of the LORD" (Is 2:5).

Nevertheless, our first parents turn away from God in the Garden of Eden (Gn 3:1–24), and the disorder introduced into the world by their sin is in spiritual and moral terms a kind of darkness. Through sin, they separate themselves from God, the Source of light. So they and their descendants are deprived of the life-giving knowledge of God.

Sin darkens their intellects, so they can no longer see God, the world, or themselves aright. "The fool walks in darkness" (Eccl 2:14). The real nature of reality becomes obscure so that the world becomes a dangerous place.

For their descendants, life becomes like a dark path across treacherous ground that must be journeyed: "They grope in the dark without light" (Jb 12:25). "They have neither knowledge nor understanding, they walk about in darkness" (Ps 82:5). "The way of the wicked is like deep darkness; they do not know over what they stumble" (Prv 4:19).

Some live as if in an underground dungeon: "Some sat in darkness and in gloom, prisoners in affliction and in irons, for they had rebelled against the words of God" (Ps 107:10–11).

Meanwhile, the wicked take advantage of the darkness as a cover for their evil deeds: "Woe to those . . . whose deeds are in the dark, and who say, 'Who sees us? Who knows us?'" (Is 29:15). "They forsake the paths of uprightness to walk in the ways of darkness, who rejoice in doing evil . . . and who are devious in their ways" (Prv 2:13–15). They "put darkness for light, and light for darkness" (Is 5:20).

THE LAW AS LIGHT

Even so, God gives his Law as a guide in the darkness, which he shines on those who seek it: "Yes, you are my lamp, O LORD, and my God lightens my darkness" (2 Sm 22:29). "Your word is a lamp to my feet, and a light to my path" (Ps 119:105). "For the commandment [of God] is a lamp and the teaching a light and the reproofs of discipline are the way of life" (Prv 6:23).

God's wisdom for living (sometimes personified as a woman in the biblical books known as "wisdom literature") is called "a reflection of eternal light. . . . She is more beautiful than the sun, and excels every constellation of the stars. Compared with the light [of the sun] she is found to be superior, for it is succeeded by the night, but against wisdom evil does not prevail" (Ws 7:26, 29–30).

Nevertheless, the Law of God is not enough to dispel

the darkness and to overcome it completely. Something, or Someone, infinitely greater than the Law is needed to come to earth and to conquer and banish the darkness. The Lord promises such a coming through the prophet Isaiah, in several Messianic prophecies.

A CHILD OF LIGHT

The first of these we have examined before, in familiar words from the scriptural lessons and music of the Christmas season: "The people who walked in darkness have seen a great light; those who dwelt in a land of deep darkness, on them has light shined. . . . For to us a child is born, to us a son is given . . ." (Is 9:2, 6).

In a later passage, God speaks through Isaiah of the same One who is to come: "Behold my servant, whom I uphold, my chosen, in whom my soul delights; I have put my Spirit upon him" (Is 42:1). The Lord then addresses this servant: "I have given you as a covenant to the people, a light to the nations, to open the eyes that are blind, to bring out the prisoners from the dungeon, from the prison those who sit in darkness" (vv. 6–7).

"I will lead the blind," the Lord continues, "in a way that they know not . . . I will turn the darkness before them into light, the rough places into level ground" (Is 42:16).

The people as a whole will be so illumined by the light God sends them that they themselves will become a light to the nations:

Arise, shine, for your light has come, and the glory
of the LORD has risen upon you, for behold, darkness
shall cover the earth, and thick darkness the peoples,

but the LORD will arise upon you, and nations shall come to your light, and kings to the brightness of your rising. . . . The sun shall be no more your light by day, nor for brightness shall the moon give light to you by night; but the LORD will be your everlasting light and your God will be your glory. (Is 60:1–3, 19)

The prophet Malachi foretells as well the coming of this light. Twice he prophesies about the coming of St. John the Baptist to prepare the way for Christ (Mal 3:1; 4:5–6; the first is quoted by our Lord in Mt 11:10, Mk 1:2; the second one he alludes to in Mt 17:11, Mk 9:12). Between these two prophecies, and after declaring that "the Lord whom you seek will suddenly come to his temple" (Mal 3:1), God promises: "For you who fear my name, the sun of righteousness shall rise, with healing in its wings" (v. 2).

"Wings" here seems to refer to the sun's beams of light, which are like wings spread out through the heavens as the sun makes its daily journey across the skies. A similar image appears in Psalm 139: "the wings of the morning" (v. 9).

THE DAWN FROM ON HIGH

As we have seen in earlier chapters, in the New Testament we find the fulfillment of the Messianic prophecies in the person of Jesus Christ. He is the Child of light, the Servant who rescues his people from darkness, the Sun of righteousness with healing in his wings. A New Testament prophet, Zechariah, first connects Jesus to this ancient imagery when he prophesies over his newborn son, John the Baptist, just months before Jesus is born:

And you, child, will be called the prophet of the Most High, for you will go before the Lord to prepare his ways [alluding to Mal 3:1, 4:5], to give knowledge of salvation to his people in the forgiveness of their sins, through the tender mercy of our God, when the day shall dawn upon us from on high [alluding to Mal 4:2] to give light to those who sit in darkness and the shadow of death [alluding to Is 9:2], to guide our feet into the way of peace. (Lk 1:76–79)

And so it happens: The One who first spoke light into the darkness, and gave his Law as a lamp for those who walked in shadows, now enters the world as Light himself.

Zechariah's reference to Christ as the dawn (in some translations, "daybreak" or "dayspring") offers us an especially lovely image. It suggests, not just the light of the sun, with all its rich meanings we have examined, but also the demise of the darkness, the beauty of a glorious sunrise, the freshness of the morning, the hope of the approaching full light of day. Dawn also recalls that supremely significant day of hope, the morning of our Lord's resurrection from the dead (Lk 24:1).

The great medieval biblical scholar Bede the Venerable (c. 672–735) comments on these words: "He found us sitting in darkness and in the shadow of death, weighed down by the ancient blindness of sins and ignorance, overcome by the deceit and the errors of the ancient enemy. . . . Our Lord brought us the true light of recognition of himself. Having taken away the darkness of errors, he opened up for us a sure way to heaven" (*Homilies on the Gospels*, 2.20).

THE LIGHT OF MEN

Zechariah's prophecy is only the first of many Gospel references to Christ as the Light. Matthew's Gospel, for example, notes that Isaiah's words "the people who sat in darkness have seen a great light" apply first to "Galilee of the Gentiles" (Mt 4:15–16). When Jesus establishes the headquarters of his ministry in that region, Matthew concludes that even this small detail of the prophecy is fulfilled in Jesus.

The first verses of John's Gospel announce Christ's coming and echo (as we saw in chapter 6) the opening lines of the book of Genesis. John speaks powerfully of Christ, the eternally existing Word of God, as the life-giving Light. "In him was life, and the life was the light of men. . . . The true light that enlightens every man was coming into the world" (Jn 1:4, 9).

Like the Old Testament writers we have noted, John also refers to the spiritual and moral darkness in a world under the domination of sin. It is a darkness pierced by the light of Christ, a darkness unable to "overcome" that light—or, depending on which of the common meanings of the Greek word here is translated, a darkness unable to "comprehend" the light. "The true light that enlightens every man was coming into the world" (Jn 1:5, 7).

John speaks of Jesus as light again in a later passage (or Jesus may be speaking of himself—in the ancient Greek original, which has no quotation marks, it is unclear where the direct quote of our Lord ends): "And this is the judgment, that the light has come into the world, and men loved darkness rather than light, because their deeds were evil. For everyone who does evil hates the light, and does not come to the light, lest his deeds should be exposed. But he who does what is true comes to the light, that it may be clearly seen that his deeds have been wrought in God" (Jn 3:19–21).

These remarks echo the words of Isaiah about those "whose deeds are in the dark, and who say, 'Who sees us? Who knows us?'" (Is 29:15).

The Light of the World

John's multiple references to Christ as the Light and the Life are unsurprising, given his report that our Lord himself once said (in another one of his famous "I AM" statements): "I am the light of the world; he who follows me will not walk in darkness, but will have the light of life" (Jn 8:12).

While the Old Testament psalmists sing of walking in the Lord's light by following his commandments, Jesus calls his disciples to follow him personally on the way to eternal life. He does not hold a lamp for them; he himself is the light. Imitating him and becoming conformed to him leads to life.

The moving story of the blind man healed by Jesus provides just one example of a pattern found in the structure of this Gospel. John often reports one of our Lord's declarations about himself, revealing his unique identity, paired with a miracle of our Lord illustrating that aspect of his identity. As we saw in chapter 4, for example, before Christ raises Lazarus from the dead, he declares, "I am the resurrection and the life" (Jn 11:25). As we saw in chapter 13, after Jesus feeds the five thousand miraculously, he declares: "I am the living bread" (Jn 6:51).

John refers to these miracles of Christ as "signs" (Jn 2:11) because their purpose is not to entertain or to attract attention to themselves. Instead, they point beyond themselves, as signs do, to something of greater importance: the true identity of Christ.

In this case, Jesus declares: "As long as I am in the world, I am the light of the world" (Jn 9:5). Then he stoops down to the ground, spits, and makes mud of the clay and the spittle. He anoints the blind man's eyes and sends him to a nearby pool to wash.

In faith, the man obeys, even though he has been blind from birth. When he comes back, he can see (Jn 9:6–7). The "sun of righteousness" has risen on this blessed man "with healing in his wings" (Mal 3:2).

SONS OF LIGHT

The theme of Christ's light appears one last time in John's Gospel when Jesus speaks about his coming death. He urges his listeners: "The light is with you for a little longer. Walk while you have the light, lest the darkness overtake you; he who walks in the darkness does not know where he goes. While you have the light, believe the light, that you may become sons of light" (Jn 12:35–36).

These words of Our Lord are parallel to John's words in the epilogue of his Gospel, where he says of the Light who came into the world: "To all who received him, who believed in his name, he gave power to become children of God" (Jn 1:9, 12). Jesus concludes: "I have come as light into the world, that whoever believes in me may not remain in darkness" (Jn 12:46).

In the teaching of the Apostle Paul, the light of Christ shines as well. St. Paul announces to the Corinthians: "For it is the God who said, 'Let light shine out of darkness' [Paul is paraphrasing Genesis here] who has shone in our hearts to give the light of the knowledge of the glory of God in the face of Christ" (2 Cor 4:6).

CHILDREN OF LIGHT

We should note that the Lord and his Apostles emphasize that those who receive his light should walk in his light and reflect his light, illumining the lives of those around. "You are the light of the world," Jesus tells his followers. "A city set on a hill cannot be hidden. Nor do men light a lamp and put it under a bushel, but on a stand, and it gives light to all in the house. Let your light so shine before men, that they may see your good works and give glory to your Father who is in heaven" (Mt 5:14–16).

Speaking of "the close of the age"—the end of the world—Jesus promises: "Then the righteous will shine like the sun in the kingdom of their Father" (Mt 13:43).

John's first epistle summarizes the life of the ones Jesus calls "children of light": "This is the message we have heard from him [the Lord] and proclaim to you, that God is light, and in him is no darkness at all. If we say we have fellowship with him while we walk in darkness, we lie and do not live according to the truth; but if we walk in the light as he is in the light, we have fellowship with one another, and the blood of Jesus his Son cleanses us from all sin" (1 Jn 1:5–7).

NO NEED OF LAMP OR SUN

As the Bible begins with God's light in the book of Genesis, so the divine light appears again at the end, in the book of Revelation.

The prophet Isaiah had once told God's people that the day would come when they would no longer need the light of the sun and moon, because the Lord himself would be their "everlasting light" (Is 60:19–20). In John's glorious vision of the heavenly Jerusalem, the eternal city of God, he echoes the ancient words of Isaiah: "The city has no need of sun or moon to shine upon it, for the glory of God is its light, and its lamp is the Lamb"—that is, the Lamb of God, Jesus Christ (Rv 21:23).

Again, in the final chapter of the Bible, we read: "And the throne of God and of the Lamb shall be in it. . . . And night shall be no more; they need no light of lamp or sun, for the Lord God will be their light" (Rv 22:3, 5). In the end, the deep and dreadful darkness of our sin is conquered by the brilliant light of God in Christ.

THE BRIGHT MORNING STAR

"In your light," the psalmist says to the Lord, "we see light" (Ps 36:9). In the light of Christ, we see God as he truly is. We see ourselves as we truly are. We see the world as it truly is.

In this light, goodness shines in all its beauty. Evil is exposed as an alluring counterfeit so that it loses its power to entice us. The darkness in our minds and hearts left by sin recedes in the presence of this light; as John's Gospel insists, the darkness cannot even understand this light, much less overcome it.

In all these ways, the light of Christ brings life to us and purifies us, just as the light of the sun is life-giving and cleansing. The Dawn from on high chases away the night, just as his resurrection from the dark tomb illumined that first Easter morning—and every morning since.

Do we fear the darkness? Are we willing to flee the darkness? We must listen, then, to the final "I AM" statement of Jesus in Scripture, declared at the close of John's vision: "I am . . . the bright morning star" (Rv 22:16).

The image of the morning star provides one last beautiful glimpse of the Lord (see also Nm 24:17; Rv 2:28; 2 Pt 1:19). In this morning star, the brilliant herald of the daybreak, we see in all his eternal radiance the Lord who is our light, our life, and our hope.

SCRIPTURAL PASSAGES TO PONDER

Genesis 1:1–3, 14–16; Wisdom 7:26, 29–30; Isaiah 9:1–2; 42:1, 6–7, 16; 60:1–3, 19–20; Malachi 4:1–3; Luke 1:76–79; John 1:4–9; 3:19–21; 8:12; 9:1–7; 12:35–36, 44–46; 2 Corinthians 4:6; Revelation 21:22–26; 22:3–5; Matthew 5:14–16; 1 John 1:5–7

> O come, thou Dayspring, come and cheer
> Our spirits by thine advent here;
> Disperse the gloomy clouds of night
> And death's dark shadows put to flight!
> Rejoice, rejoice! Emmanuel
> Shall come to thee, O Israel!
>
> FROM "O COME, O COME EMMANUEL"

17

Pioneer and Perfecter
of Our Faith

*Looking to Jesus, the pioneer
and perfecter of our faith.*

HEBREWS 12:2

Growing up in Georgia, I learned the three-word motto that appears on the "Great Seal" of the State: "Wisdom, Justice, Moderation."

Years later in college, I discovered why these words were chosen. We learned about the four cardinal virtues as taught by the ancient Greek philosophers, and the Fathers of the Church as well. These virtues are wisdom (or prudence), justice, moderation (or temperance), and fortitude. But one of these four is missing from the Georgia state seal: the virtue of fortitude.

That seal reminds me how today, fortitude is often a neglected virtue. That's one reason why a look at Jesus as the Pioneer and Perfecter of our faith is so important. In this powerful portrait, we learn from our Lord the necessity of a persevering faith.

214

RUNNING THE RACE

The athlete has long served as a vivid biblical image of the man or woman striving and struggling for holiness. Jacob wrestles with God (Gn 32:24–30). The Apostle Paul sees himself as a spiritual boxer who must toughen himself to endure the blows of the adversary (1 Cor 9:26). St. Timothy is urged to be a good fighter (1 Tm 6:12) and a soldier well-disciplined as an athlete who follows the rules of the competition (1 Tm 2:1–11; 4:6–8).

The most common of such biblical images, however, is that of the runner. This particular athletic endeavor functions well as a symbol of the life of faithfulness and holiness, when the race that is undertaken is understood more as a marathon than a sprint.

At times the course seems too steep, too long, or too dangerous. The runner feels too weak to run or too tired to continue. Perhaps an injury or disability makes progress difficult if not impossible.

At other times, the course seems uncertain, poorly marked, and confusing. The way to go may be obscured by darkness. The runner may thus lose his way—or he may simply fail to finish the race because of compelling distractions that pull him off the course.

THE WAY OF FAITHFULNESS AND WISDOM

The psalmist entreats God to keep him on the right course, and he rejoices that God's commandments show him where to run. "Put false ways far from me, and graciously teach me your law! I have chosen the way of faithfulness, I set your ordinances before me.... I will run in the way of your commandments ... Teach me, O LORD, the way of your statutes, and I will keep it to the end" (Ps 119:29–33).

The faithful runner refuses to allow distractions to turn him aside from the race: "Incline my heart to your testimonies, and not to your gain! Turn my eyes from looking at vanities, and give me life in your ways" (Ps 119:36–37).

In the book of Proverbs, a father exhorts his son to follow the way of wisdom if he hopes to receive "a beautiful crown" (Prv 4:9). "I have led you in the paths of uprightness," he reminds the young man.

If the youth remains on the course marked out instead of entering in "the path of the wicked ... the way of evil men" (Prv 4:14), he is sure to succeed: "When you walk, your step will not be hampered; and if you run, you will not stumble. ... The path of the righteous is like the light of dawn, which shines brighter and brighter until full day" (vv. 12, 18).

If he runs contrary to God's commandments, however, he will be running on a dark, dangerous track on uneven ground, filled with unseen obstacles: "The way of the wicked is like deep darkness; they do not know over what they stumble" (Prv 4:19).

For this reason, the young man running the race must not wander off the right track; he must set his eyes on the goal ahead: "Let your eyes look directly forward, and your gaze be straight before you. Take heed to the path of your feet, then all your ways will be sure. Do not swerve to the right or to the left; turn your foot away from evil" (Prv 4:25–27).

The father's concern that his son complete the course is mirrored by God's own desire for the young man to be morally and spiritually fit. He trains and disciplines him to prepare for the challenge: "My son, do not despise the LORD's discipline or be weary of his reproof, for the LORD reproves him whom he loves, as a father the son in whom he delights" (Prv 3:11–12).

"THEY SHALL RUN AND NOT BE WEARY"

For his part, the prophet Isaiah announces a stirring exhortation to perseverance in terms of athletic training and encouragement: "Strengthen the weak hands, and make firm the feeble knees. Say to those who are of a fearful heart, 'Be strong, fear not! Behold, your God . . . will come and save you'" (Is 35:3–4).

Later in the same book, the Lord offers powerful consolation to those who are in danger of giving up on the race: "Have you not known? Have you not heard? The LORD is the everlasting God, the Creator of the ends of the earth. He does not faint or grow weary; his understanding is unsearchable" (Is 40:28).

Yet the Lord is not just the exemplar of strength and stamina, the prophet declares. As the very source of those qualities, he provides us the gift of fortitude: "He gives power to the faint, and to him who has no might he increases strength. Even youths shall faint and be weary, and young men shall fall exhausted, but they who wait for the LORD shall renew their strength, they shall mount up with wings like eagles, they shall run and not be weary, they shall walk and not be faint" (Is 40:29–31).

In all these passages, the emphasis is on divine grace. God's gracious gift of health and strength enables those who are weak and weary to endure and finish the race. Such encouragement will much later be echoed by the Lord's consolation to the Apostle Paul: "My grace is sufficient for you, for my power is made perfect in weakness" (2 Cor 12:9).

AN IMPERISHABLE WREATH

In the New Testament, St. Paul enthusiastically embraces the image of the Christian life as a challenging race, drawing his imagery especially from the Greek and Roman games familiar to Christian converts from pagan cultures. For example, he asks the Corinthians: "Do you not know that in a race all the runners compete, but only one receives the prize? So run that you may obtain it. Every athlete exercises self-control in all things. They do it to receive a perishable wreath, but we an imperishable. . . . I do not run aimlessly" (1 Cor 9:24–26).

The "wreath" he notes is of course the laurel wreath given to the winner of Greek and Roman athletic competitions.

Paul also urges the Philippian Christians under his pastoral care to remain "blameless and innocent" so that on Judgment Day ("the day of Christ"), he can be proud that he did not "run in vain" (Phil 2:16).

When the Galatians get off track spiritually, Paul reproves them as competitors losing a race: "You were running well; who hindered you from obeying the truth?" (Gal 5:7).

At the end of his life, the Apostle declares: "I have fought the good fight, I have finished the race, I have kept the faith. Henceforth there is laid up for me the crown of righteousness, which the Lord, the righteous judge, will award to me on that [Judgment] Day, and not only to me but also to all who have loved his appearing" (2 Tm 4:7–8). In this depiction of the Christian life, the reward of a laurel wreath (eternal life) is awarded at the finish line (Judgment Day) by the judge of the competition (the Lord).

"I PRESS ON"

In chapter 1, we noted how the Apostle exhorted the Philippians to a faithful endurance (Phil 3). We can revisit that passage now with a focus on his use of athletic imagery for the Christian life. The Apostle paints a powerful self-portrait as the runner who perseveres (3:12–16). He urges the Philippians to make his fortitude a model for their own: "Brethren, join in imitating me, and mark those who so live as you have an example in us" (v. 17).

What lessons can we learn from Paul's experience? As we have seen, we learn that the only goal of life's race that is worth attaining in life is Christ himself. "Whatever gain I had, I counted as loss for the sake of Christ" (Phil 3:7).

St. John Chrysostom comments on the Apostle's words:

Look upward, where the prize is; the sight of the prize strengthens the determination of our will. The hope of taking it keeps us from even noticing the labor involved; it makes the distance appear short. And what is this prize? No palm branch; but what? The kingdom of heaven, everlasting rest, glory together with Christ, the inheritance, brotherhood, ten thousand good things, which it is impossible to name. It is impossible to describe the beauty of that prize; only he who has it knows it, and he who is about to receive it.

This matchless prize, St. John concludes, "is not of gold, it is not set with jewels, it is far more precious. Gold is mud, in comparison with that prize; precious stones are mere bricks in comparison with its beauty" (*Homily on Philippians,* 12.3.14).

According to Paul, "becoming like him [Jesus]" in his suffering, death, and resurrection is the finish line of the race, a destination that Paul has not yet reached: "Not that I have already obtained this or am already perfect, but I press on to make it my own" (Phil 3:10–12).

We also learn that having fellowship with Christ is the reward for running the race: "Indeed I count everything as loss because of the surpassing worth of knowing Christ Jesus my Lord . . . because Christ Jesus has made me his own" (Phil 3:8, 12).

The race has cost the Apostle everything, yet he counts the reward well worth the cost: "For his sake I have suffered the loss of all things, and count them as refuse, in order that I may gain Christ and be found in him . . . that I may know him" (Phil 3:8–10).

Paul teaches us as well to avoid distractions. As a determined athlete, he must focus intently on the goal of the race, not allowing himself to be distracted or turned aside: "One thing I do, forgetting what lies behind and straining forward to what lies ahead, I press on toward the goal for the prize of the upward call of God in Christ Jesus" (Phil 3:13–14).

St. John Chrysostom notes: "He [Paul] says not simply 'I run' but 'I press on.' Consider how the pursuer strains in his pursuit. He sees nothing, he thrusts away all who impede him with great force, he cherishes his mind, his eye, his strength, his soul, and his body, looking at nothing other than the crown" (*Homily on Philippians,* 12.3.12).

JESUS AS OUR MODEL ATHLETE

In this exhortation, Paul urges his readers to imitate him as he runs the race. But we should note how he assumes that he himself can be a model only because Jesus is his own model: "Be imitators of me," he tells the Corinthians, "as I am of Christ" (1 Cor 11:1). The closer Paul gets to the goal, the more closely he imitates Christ, "becoming like him" (Phil 3:10).

The book of Hebrews focuses on Christ as our model for running the good race of faith, especially in the face of struggle, suffering, hostility, and other adversity (Heb 10:32–34; 12:3–4). He has run the race and is now "crowned with glory and honor because of the suffering of death, so that by the grace of God he might taste death for everyone. . . . For it was fitting that he [God] . . . in bringing many sons to glory, should make the pioneer of their salvation perfect through suffering" (Heb 2:9–10).

The passion and death of Christ as he ran the race make possible our glorious salvation as the conclusion of our race. He was made "perfect" through his suffering—not in the sense that he was morally imperfect and needed refining, but in the sense that he was brought to the completion of his race and fulfillment of his mission through his suffering and death. Because he has "tasted death" for us all, he can now bring to final glory those who run the race after him and through him, who themselves must be brought to the completion of their mission through suffering and death.

THE PIONEER

For this reason, Christ is the "pioneer" of our salvation. The Greek word *aitios* that is translated here as "pioneer" means literally "the source, the cause," of our salvation. The glorious reward of eternal life that awaits us at the end of our race finds its origin in him. The English translation "pioneer" evokes the image of someone taking us into new territory—the Promised Land.

The author of Hebrews goes on to urge us to a steadfast faith, "the assurance of things hoped for, the conviction of things not seen" (Heb 11:1). We might view it as a trusting confidence in God that he desires, and has made possible, the successful conclusion of our race, even if the finish line is not yet in sight. To inspire us to cultivate such faith, he provides what some have called "the roll call of faith"—a list of holy men and women who ran the race with a firm faith (Heb 11:4–39).

At this point, the imagery of running the race becomes explicit. "Therefore, since we are surrounded by so great a cloud of witnesses, let us also lay aside every weight, and sin which clings so closely, and let us run with perseverance the race that is set before us" (Heb 12:1). The saints who have run the race before us are now like spectators in the stadium who watch as we run the race, cheering us on to the goal.

Sin is like a weight that slows us down; we must cast off every disordered attachment that would hinder us. The key to completing the race is to follow in the footsteps of Christ himself, focusing on the One without sin, relying on his gracious assistance: "Looking to Jesus the pioneer and perfecter of our faith" (Heb 12:2).

Here a different Greek word is translated by the English term "pioneer." The Greek *archegos* means literally the chief leader, the captain, the prince. The "pioneer" of our salvation is also the "pioneer" of our faith—the one who leads us to the goal as our captain and king by inspiring our faith in him.

THE PERFECTER

Yet Christ is not only our "pioneer," the source of our salvation, our leader and example in faith. He is also our "perfecter" (Heb 12:2). The Greek term here is *teleiotes,* derived from the word *telos,* which means "end, conclusion, goal." Christ is the One who perfects and completes us, who brings us to our goal—the One who causes us to finish the race and accomplish our mission. Looking to him, we receive grace and strength and power.

Christ's endurance must become the pattern of our own. And how did he endure? "For the joy that was set before him, [he] endured the cross, despising the shame, and is seated at the right hand of the throne of God" (Heb 12:2).

What was the joy set before him that inspired such endurance? His joyful return to "the right hand" of his Father in glory. John tells us in his Gospel that on the night Jesus was betrayed, he was able to "love them [his disciples] to the end"—that is, he was able to endure his passion and give his life for them—because "he knew that his hour had come to depart out of this world to the Father." He knew "that he had come from God and was going to God" (Jn 13:1, 3).

"Consider him who endured from sinners such hostility against himself, so that you may not grow weary or fainthearted" (Heb 12:3). The words echo the prophet Isaiah's encouragement to God's people that those who look to the Lord "shall run and not be weary, they shall walk and not faint" (Is 40:31).

Then the author quotes the passage from Proverbs we have noted about avoiding discouragement when God disciplines us. He does it for our good, as a father disciplines his children (Prv 3:11–12). The Greek word here for discipline, *paideia*, means not just correction, but training—in this case, training to run the race. "Therefore lift your drooping hands and strengthen your weak knees, and make straight paths for your feet, so that what is lame may not be put out of joint but rather be healed" (Heb 12:12).

In all these ways, our successful completion of the race of this life depends utterly on Jesus. He is the Source of the salvation that makes the race possible, and the Reward that awaits us at the end. Between the beginning and the end, he is the One who trains us, leads us, inspires us, takes us to the goal—"the pioneer and perfecter of our faith."

SCRIPTURAL PASSAGES TO PONDER

Proverbs 3:1–12; 4:10–12; Isaiah 35:3–4; 40:27–31; Philippians 2:14–16; 3:12–16; 1 Corinthians 9:24–27; 2 Timothy 2:1–11; 4:6–8; Hebrews 12:1–16

> *Awake, my soul, stretch every nerve,*
> *And press with vigor on!*
> *A heavenly race demands thy zeal,*
> *And an immortal crown.*
> *Blest Savior, introduced by thee,*
> *have I my race begun;*
> *And, crowned with victory at thy feet,*
> *I'll lay my honors down.*

FROM PHILIP DODDERIDGE, "AWAKE, MY SOUL, STRETCH EVERY NERVE"

18

ALPHA AND OMEGA

*I am the Alpha and the Omega, the first
and the last, the beginning and the end.*

REVELATION 22:13

Through some of his biblical names and titles, we have now begun—but only just begun—to paint a rich and detailed portrait of Jesus Christ. The last title to be considered comes from the first and last letters of the Greek alphabet, *alpha* and *omega*. It provides an appropriate final glimpse of our Lord, because it points to his role in history, and in the life of every believer, as "the first and the last, the beginning and the end" (Rv 22:13).

In an historical sense, Jesus Christ is the first and the last. The eternal Son of God set human history into motion through the creation of the human race. He will bring human history to a close when he returns in glory to judge the living and the dead.

Yet at an even deeper level, Jesus Christ is the beginning and the end. He is both the Origin, the very Source, of creation, and the Goal, the Destiny, of creation; for he has made us for himself.

"DECLARING THE END FROM THE BEGINNING"

"I am God, and there is no other; I am God, and there is none like me, declaring the end from the beginning. . . . I have spoken, and I will bring it to pass; I have planned, and I will do it" (Is 46:9–11). Throughout Scripture, the voice of the great I AM speaks to us from eternity, from beyond the universe of time and space he has created, revealing himself and his plan for the human race he loves.

Through the prophet Isaiah especially, the voice of God thunders, reminding his people that he has no rivals as the Lord of time and eternity: "Thus says the LORD, the King of Israel and his Redeemer, the LORD of hosts: 'I am the first and I am the last; besides me, there is no god. Who is like me? . . . Is there a God besides me? . . . Listen to me, O Jacob, and Israel, whom I called! I am He; I am the first, and I am the last" (Is 44:6–8; 48:12).

St. Cyril of Alexandria remarks on this passage: "For God is the first principle, the beginning of the universe. He himself has no beginning, and through him everything has been brought into being. He himself did not come into being by some agent; rather, he is and will be. For this is his very name ["I am who I am," Ex 3:14] and his eternal remembrance unto ages of ages" (*Commentary on Isaiah,* 44:2–7).

The psalmists praise the Lord for his eternal nature: "Lord, you have been our dwelling place in all generations, before the mountains were brought forth, or ever you had formed the earth and the world, from everlasting to everlasting you are God" (Ps 90:1–2). "Blessed be the Lord, the God of Israel, from everlasting to everlasting! Amen and amen" (Ps 41:13). "Your throne is established from of old; you are from everlasting" (Ps 93:2).

CHRIST, THE ALPHA AND OMEGA

"Before Abraham was, I am" (Jn 8:58). As we saw in chapter 7, Jesus Christ is in fact the eternal "I AM." Existing outside of time, God has nevertheless entered into time, taking his place in human history as One of us, calling us to himself as our eternal Home. Jesus Christ, the God-Man, stands at the center of history, yet he also brought about history's beginning and awaits us at its end.

We see this reality displayed clearly in the book of Revelation, with its riveting vision of history's end and of heaven's eternity. As we have found, Christ reveals himself to John again and again under various titles: Son of man, Lamb, Lion of the tribe of Judah, First-born of the dead, Root and Offspring of David, bright morning Star, Lord of lords and King of kings, and more. But one particular title that appears throughout the book echoes the "first and last" declaration of Isaiah and the psalmists' praise of the One who is "everlasting." That title is "the Alpha and the Omega."

In Greek, the language in which the New Testament is written, alpha is the first letter of the alphabet, and omega is the last. To speak of the Lord as "the alpha and the omega" is similar to saying in English that he is "everything from A to Z." All things are from him and for him.

Tertullian (c. 155–c. 240), a third-century African

Christian writer, puts it this way: "The Lord applied to himself two Greek letters, the first and the last, as figures of the beginning and the end, which are united in himself. For just as alpha continues on until it reaches omega, and omega completes the cycle again back to alpha, so he meant to show us that in him is found the course of all things from the beginning to the end, and from the end back to the beginning" (*On Monogamy,* 5).

We hear this title first in the opening passage of the book, even before John recalls the details of the vision. He writes: "'I am the Alpha and the Omega,' says the Lord God, who is and who was and who is to come, the Almighty" (Rv 1:8). The latter part of this statement refers to God in the present, in the past, and in the future, much like the psalmist's words: "from everlasting [past] to everlasting [future], you are God [present]" (Ps 90:1–2).

Here John attributes the title to the Almighty God, the One beyond all time. But soon, "one like a Son of Man" stands before him in human form, and he makes a startling claim: "I am the first and the last, and the living one; I died, and behold I am alive for evermore" (Rv 1:17–18). The "Son of man" is of course Jesus. John reports that Jesus tells him to write "the words of the first and last, who died and came to life" (2:8). As Jesus speaks to John, he applies to himself the words that were used by God to identify himself when he spoke through Isaiah.

In a later chapter, John tells us that Jesus, seated on his throne in heaven, identifies himself this way again: "He said to me, 'It is done! I am the Alpha and the Omega, the beginning and the end'" (Rv 21:1–7). Then in the closing passage of the book, Jesus declares: "Behold, I am coming soon. . . . I am the

Alpha and the Omega, the first and the last, the beginning and the end" (22:12–14).

THE FRAMEWORK OF HISTORY

In the book of Revelation, consider further two phrases closely connected with the title "Alpha and Omega" as the Lord speaks to John: He says he is "the First and the Last" (Rv 22:13) and the One "who is, and who was, and who is to come" (Rv 1:8). In these added statements, we find a profound historical dimension.

The overarching theme of the book of Revelation is that history is working its way to a glorious conclusion, a conclusion planned and ordained from the very first. And at the beginning, the end, and the center of that history stands Someone who is the key to understanding it all: the Lord Jesus Christ.

Jesus of Nazareth, a man who was born on the earth only two thousand years ago, is nevertheless "the Alpha," "the First" historically, because he is God in the flesh, the One who in the beginning set history, the story of the human race, into motion. In light of the opening lines in John's Gospel especially, we can understand why Jesus calls himself "the Alpha," "the first," "the beginning." He is the eternal Word, who "was in the beginning with God" before all time (Jn 1:2). In addition, "all things were made through him" (Jn 1:3). All creation, and human history in particular, begins as his handiwork.

In what sense, then, is Jesus "the Omega," "the last," "the end"? The One who stands at the beginning of creation and of human history also stands at its conclusion. As we have seen in numerous biblical passages, Jesus will return one day to draw history to an end and to judge the human race (Jn 5:26–29; Mt 25:31–46). The Nicene Creed summarizes this truth in this way: "He will come again in glory to judge the living and the dead, and his kingdom will have no end."

So the One "who is" (Jesus of Nazareth) and "who was" (the Creator in the beginning) is the same One "who is to come"—the cosmic Lord returning to conquer and reign. He will draw the curtain on human history; he will bring to a close the age-old human story. The First is the Last; and the Last is the First.

When Jesus says, then, that he is "the Alpha and the Omega," he's revealing himself as the very Framework of history, who stands at its beginning as well as its end, encompassing the whole within himself. When we ask, "Where did the human race come from? Where is it going?" Christ replies: "It began in me, and it will end in me."

FIRST CAUSE AND FINAL CAUSE

Yet there is more meaning still to be plumbed in this mystery. Jesus isn't content to call himself only "the Alpha and the Omega, the First and the Last." He must add as well that he is "the Beginning and the End."

Now we might be tempted to think that Our Lord is merely repeating the idea for emphasis. But a look at the New Testament Greek words here suggests a far deeper reality. Their meanings point us beyond the merely historical dimension to a more foundational one—at the level of our very being.

Long before John recorded his vision, even some of the pagan Greek thinkers—without any special revelations from God—had reasoned their way to certain basic truths about

the world. The celebrated philosopher Aristotle, for example, had figured out that behind everything in the cosmos
must stand the "Unmoved Mover," as he put it: the primary,
the fundamental, Cause of everything else that is, which has
no cause Itself. This universal Mover, as the Cause behind all
other causes, he called the "First Cause."

More remarkable still was Aristotle's insistence that
the cosmic First Cause was also what he called the "Final
Cause." That is, the philosopher claimed that things were
"caused"—moved, shaped, determined—to a great extent by
their purpose, by their destiny, by what they were intended to
be. This "Final Cause" is like the DNA within an organism:
Present from the beginning, it causes the organism to grow in
a certain way, to mature into a certain thing, the thing it was
ordained to become.

As Christians, of course, we understand that both the First
Cause and the Final Cause are God. He is the Creator who,
like a great magnet, draws all things to himself. The natural
goodness in all things loves and yearns for perfection—loves
and yearns for God, whether or not they realize it. So God is
both the Source and the intended Destiny of everything that is.

The Greek terms in Revelation translated "beginning"
and "end" reflect this deep level of meaning. *Arche,* "beginning," means in this context more than simply "the start."
It signifies the origin, the foundational principle—the First
Cause. Christ is the very Source of all things.

Telos, on the other hand, doesn't mean "end" in the sense
of ceasing to be. Instead, as we saw in the previous chapter,
it is "end" in the sense of the purpose for which something
exists, the goal toward which it is striving—the Final Cause.

Jesus, then, is not only the divine Judge whose return to

earth brings about "the close of the age" (Mt 28:20). He is also "the Omega," "the last," "the end" in the sense that all creation—and, in a privileged way, those of the human race who are redeemed—finds its destiny in him. Christ is our *telos:* our conclusion, its consummation, the intended goal for which we were created.

Seen in this light, Christ's claim to be "the Alpha and the Omega" should pierce us to our very depths. He didn't just make us. He is, from moment to moment, our very Source, the Ground of our existence. That's the "Alpha" end of the mystery.

But the "Omega" end of the mystery is just as awesome. It's not just that Jesus Christ, God the Son, made us. He made us for a *purpose*. And what is that purpose? *He made us for himself.*

He's not only the Soil in which we grow; he's the Sunlight for which we reach. We spring from his love as Creator; we blossom and bear fruit in his love as Redeemer. He himself is our Purpose, our Perfection.

"FIRST-BORN OF ALL CREATION"

St. Paul peers more deeply into this mystery in his epistles. Writing to the Colossians, in the opening section of his letter he presents a lyrical passage, followed by commentary, which is essentially a hymn (Col 1:15–20). Biblical scholars have debated whether Paul wrote the hymn himself or is simply quoting and commenting on a hymn of the early Church that his readers would recognize. Either way, the passage sings high praise to Christ as the origin and goal of all things.

First, Paul refers to Christ's role in creation: "He is the

image of the invisible God, the first-born of all creation; for in him, all things were created in heaven and on earth, visible and invisible" (Col 1:15–16). We should note here that "the first-born of all creation" does not suggest that Jesus is himself a creature, the first of creatures, the "eldest child" of a family. The statement that follows, "in him, all things were created"—not to mention the rest of the Apostle's teaching about Christ—rules out that interpretation.

The term "first-born" is used throughout the Old Testament (130 times), usually to indicate priority in time and sovereignty of rank. The word also frequently designates the son who has first place in his father's heart and was used to speak both of the Messiah and of personified Wisdom (Ps 89:27; Prv 8:24–25).

THE ORIGINAL WISDOM

In chapter 6 we talked about the passages in the Old Testament that personify Wisdom, speaking of Wisdom's role in creation, and we noted that this portrait seems to lie behind John's teaching about Christ as the Word of God. In his first letter to the Corinthians, Paul identifies Christ with that Wisdom (1 Cor 1:24), and the Old Testament portrait seems to lie behind these words to the Colossians as well.

There, Wisdom is said to be an "image" of God's goodness (Ws 7:26) that existed "at the first, before the beginning of the earth" (Prv 8:23). Wisdom is actively involved in the world's creation, "beside him [God] like a master workman" (Prv 8:30). The parallels between the Old Testament portraits of Wisdom and Paul's praise of Christ are clear.

The Apostle next specifies some of the elements of the

"invisible creation" that came into being through Christ's divine agency—"thrones or dimensions or principalities or authorities" (Col 1:16). These terms refer to angelic ranks (Rom 8:38; Eph 1:21; 3:10, 6:12; Col 2:15), and given the situation in the city of Colossae, the Apostle is probably speaking of fallen angels. At the time, heretical teachers are infiltrating the community, and apparently they claim that "elemental spirits of the universe," demonic powers, are at work to control the human race. Paul is reminding his readers that Christ is sovereign over these tyrannical spirits.

Yet the Apostle's declarations about the supremacy of Christ are more exalted still. Not only were all things created "through him"; they were created "for him" (Col 1:16, emphasis added). "All things" created move toward him as their goal, their *telos,* just as we have heard in our Lord's words to John in the book of Revelation (Rv 22:12).

"IN HIM ALL THINGS HOLD TOGETHER"

Even so, Paul tells us, there is more. "He is before all things, and *in him all things hold together*" (Col 1:17, emphasis added). The universe not only has its beginning and end in Christ; its ongoing existence is utterly dependent on him.

The world is established in Christ as a foundation. He sustains all creation, unifies it, keeps it in existence. If not for his continuing act of cohesive power, all things would fall apart, disintegrate, dissolve into nothingness. The writer of Hebrews echoes these words, announcing that God's Son is "the heir of all things, through whom also he created the ages," God's image who "bears the very stamp of his nature, *upholding the universe by his word of power*" (Heb 1:2–3, emphasis added).

"In him all the fullness of God was pleased to dwell" (Col 1:29). As God himself, Christ cannot be other than the beginning, the end, and the power uniting all things. Having become a Man, through his sacrifice—"the blood of his cross"—he reconciles to himself "all things, whether on earth or in heaven" (Col 1:19–20). Though sin has brought disorder, fragmentation, and alienation to the world, Christ's redemptive work restores order, unity, and coherence.

Paul teaches the Ephesians in similar words. God's "plan for the fullness of time," he insists, is "to unite all things in him [Christ], things in heaven and things on earth" (Eph 1:10). The fourth-century writer Maurinus Victorinus sums up that passage in this way: "He [Christ] is salvation; he is renewal; he is eternity" (*Commentary on Ephesians*, 1.1.10).

"ALL IN ALL"

Again, writing to the Corinthians, the Apostle announces that, uniting all things within himself, in the end God the Son will unite himself in loving submission to God the Father, bringing with him all things (1 Cor 15:28). The goal is "that God may be everything to everyone" (v. 28); or to render the text as most translations do—more literally and with a vision grander still—"that God may be all in all" (Douay-Rheims Version; New American Bible).

The third-century African theologian Origen reads this passage in light of a reality we discussed in chapter 10, the Beatific Vision—that vision of God, face-to-face, which grants those in heaven perfect blessedness, the ultimate happiness.

John's first epistle tells us: "Beloved, we are God's children now; it does not yet appear what we shall be, but we know that when he appears, we shall be like him, for we shall see him as he is" (1 Jn 3:2).

St. Paul also speaks of finally seeing God in heaven "face to face" (1 Cor 13:12). We were created for that final vision, designed to be united in perfect love with the One who is our Alpha and our Omega, our first and our last, our beginning and our end. In our heart of hearts, whether or not we realize it, we are all among "those who seek him, who seek the face of . . . God" (Ps 24:6).

Origen writes: "God will be all things in each human being in such a manner that everything that the reasoning mind can feel or understand or think will be all God. . . . That mind will think of God and see God and hold God. God will be the manner and measure of its every movement. In this way, God will be all in all" (*On First Principles,* 3.6.3).

In the Beatific Vision, St. Augustine concludes, "God will be the consummation of all our desiring—the object of our unending vision, of our undiminishing love, of our unwearying praise. And in this gift of vision, the response of love, this hymn of praise, all will share alike, as all will share in everlasting life" (*City of God,* 22.30). What higher destiny, what greater glory, could we possible desire?

"I AM"

As we come to the close of this study of the names and titles of Jesus in Scripture, we must reflect on this profound truth. When Jesus reveals himself as "the Alpha and the Omega," he answers some of the deepest questions of the human heart:

"Where did we come from? Where are we going? What is our origin? What is our destiny? Why are we here?"

The reply to all these questions comes thundering from heaven: "I AM. *I* AM the Way, the Truth, and the Life. *I* AM the Alpha and the Omega, the first and the last, the beginning and the end. *I* AM Jesus Christ. Come, follow me. I have made you for myself, and I will take you home."

SCRIPTURAL PASSAGES TO PONDER

Isaiah 44:6–8; 46:9–11; 48:12–13; Psalms 90:1–2; Revelation 1:8, 17–18; 21:1–7; 22:12–14; Colossians 1:15–20; Hebrews 1:1–3; 1 John 3:1–3

Of the Father's love begotten,
Ere the worlds began to be
He is Alpha and Omega,
He the Source, the Ending he,
Of the things that are, that have been,
And eternal years shall be,
Evermore and evermore!
Christ to Thee, with God the Father,
And, O Holy Ghost, to Thee
Hymn and chant and high thanksgiving
And unwearied praises be:
Honor, glory, and dominion,
And eternal victory,
Evermore and evermore!

FROM AURELIUS CLEMENS PRUDENTIUS,
"OF THE FATHER'S LOVE BEGOTTEN"